12586

P9-EEN-206

Standing by Words

Essays by Wendell Berry

North Point Press
San Francisco
1983

Some of these essays were published in somewhat different
form in the following periodicals, to which the author and
publisher wish to express their thanks: *Hudson Review*
("The Specialization of Poetry," "Standing by Words"),
Lindisfarne ("Standing by Words"), *Resurgence* ("People,
Land, and Community"), *Sierra Club Bulletin* ("People,
Land, and Community"), *CoEvolution Quarterly* ("Poetry
and Marriage").

For Gary Snyder

Contents

Standing by Words

1

The Specialization of Poetry (1974)

For some time I have been gathering and reading a number of examples of the newest of literary genres, the interview-with-a-poet. I have at hand interviews with Philip Levine, James Dickey, Galway Kinnell, William Matthews, Adrienne Rich, Anne Sexton, Louis Simpson, and Mark Strand. At first I was mainly curious about the reasons for the growth of this genre: What does it mean that the work habits, personal circumstances, and casual opinions of poets have come to be held in such regard by the editors of magazines, by at least some readers, and evidently by the poets themselves? But the interviewed poets were expressing ideas that have been common in writings and discussions of poetry for a good many years, and as I read I saw how several of these ideas work together to define a specialization of poetry similar to the specialization of other disciplines.

My understanding of this specialization of poetry is, of course, indebted to the work of many writers. The subject has been dealt with most ably, among writings known to me, in John Crowe Ransom's essay, "Poets without Laurels," and in Edwin Muir's lucid book, *The Estate of Poetry*. Ransom spoke of the purification or the puritanization of poetry, which he saw as a part of the general dissociation of the "elements of experience" and of the "faculties" of the modern mind, and Muir of the diminishment of poetry's "estate," which he defined as its "effective range and influence." The Ransom essay was published in

The World's Body in 1938, when the catastrophe of dissociation was still in its adolescence. *The Estate of Poetry* comprises the Charles Eliot Norton Lectures delivered by Muir in 1955–56. By then the dissociation of which Ransom wrote had produced a working model of Doomsday, and though Muir's book is not apocalyptic it is informed by the historical urgency that burdens his later poems. Applied science (not necessarily "applied" by scientists) had had its tour de force in World War II, and Muir had understood the ferocious logic that was upon us.

Because of the proliferation of so-called protest poetry and the widespread involvement of poets in public issues after about 1964, it became possible to suppose that the concerns of Ransom and Muir had become somewhat dated. For a while during the sixties I hoped, and even believed, that the effort of many poets to speak out against public outrages might recover some of the lost estate of poetry; and I think that I was by no means the only one who hoped and believed this. But the political "involvement" of poets appears now to have subsided, leaving the "effective range and influence" of poetry no larger than before.

Having had several years in which to write my own protests, and several more in which to consider them and their effect, I conclude that I was wrong. I do not mean that I feel the protests to have been wrong, or that I would not—or that I do not now—protest the outrages that I know to be taking place. I was wrong in assuming that protest, in itself, might alter the status of poetry.

The primary aspect of specialization is practical; the specialist withdraws from responsibility for everything not comprehended by his specialty. Each specialization, Ransom says, "has had to resist the insidious charms of aesthetic experience before its own perfection could arise." But this is a perfection of a kind never before contemplated in human history—a perfection that depends upon the abandonment of all the old ideals of harmony, symmetry, balance, order, in favor of the singular totalitarian ideal of control, which is typically achieved by leaving out or discounting or destroying whatever is not subject to control. Our achievement of this sort of control over certain particles of the Creation has given rise to the supposition that such control is possible on a much grander scale, which would permit us to bring nature and history into line with our intentions. There is no need, I think, to dwell on the moral degeneracy, the spiritual misery, the abuses and wastes of power that are the result of this ambition. And we are every day surrounded by more evidence of its futility. Human control on any grand scale is impossible, and the technological and political controls that *are* possible are frequently the opposite of order; any viable human order must come to terms with the impossibility of absolute control.

Engineering, agriculture, and other practical disciplines, then, shrugged off the claims of esthetics—among other things. Their withdrawal from the concern for esthetics defined that as the proper "field" for artists. And the artists specialized their various disciplines, Ransom says, by breaking down "the union of beauty with goodness and truth, "which until then was "common enough to be regarded as natural." In reaction to the utilitarianism of other disciplines, the arts became defiantly nonutilitarian.

Ransom's version of the modern role of the poet undoubtedly needs to be amended somewhat. First it must be made to accommodate his own obvious concern with the larger responsibilities of poets—likewise that of Allen Tate, one of whose poems Mr. Ransom cites as an example of the "obscure" or unmoral poem. One must mention such self-consciously "national" poets as Yeats, Williams, and MacDiarmid, and a poet so determinedly a teacher as Pound; one knows that some poets have resisted the claims of beauty and that others have attempted to be moralists or mages or priests or politicians. So much said, it remains true that the poet is isolated and specialized and that the old union of beauty, goodness, and truth is broken. It remains true that, as Muir said, "The public has become one of the subjects of poetry, but is no longer its audience."

I believe that the sudden rise and growth of the interview genre is itself a symptom of the specialization of poetry, and that it reveals some of the dangers. It suggests, as a sort of implied premise, that poets are different from other people; hence the interest in what they *say* as opposed to what they write. (The popularity of poetry readings, which about parallels the vogue of the interview, probably owes something to the same feeling, though the readings have a more legitimate function.) There has come to be a class of what might be called poet watchers, who seem to be convinced that, whereas their own lives are routine and dull, the lives of poets are constantly "different" and exciting. Judging from their tone and their lack of controversy, I conclude that most interviews with poets are conducted by poet watchers. The purpose cannot be a dialogue between two beings of the same general kind; that, surely, would lead to hard questions or, better, to argument. Nor can the purpose be to learn what the poets have to say about their art, for that could be better done in an essay; if it is to be done at all, it ought to be done in an essay. The idea, obviously, is to *examine* the poet, to study as unobtrusively as possible whatever privacies may be disclosed by the inadvertences of conversation. The interviewer operates in a blind of obsequiousness, hoping the poets will reveal themselves as the strange creatures they *really* are. The interviewers and their intended readers are so convinced of the poet's otherness that they need to stand in his presence and say, "Well, well, so this is a poet." At a poetry reading once, I sat behind a group of such spectators who passed back and forth during the entire evening a huge pair of binoculars.

But poet watchers have a limitation in common with bird watchers. Some essential things will not be revealed to them, because their interest is too direct, too imbued with the excitement of a special occasion. They are too much agog. If to an attentiveness appropriately critical and calm the words of a poet reveal something extraordinary, then an extraordinary response is certainly in order. But it is better to be agape afterwards than agog beforehand.

The poet watcher is a kind of absurdity. But insofar as they have helped to create him and to the degree that they indulge or exploit or need his excitement, there is also an absurdity in poets. There is apparently now some widespread feeling among poets themselves that they are of a different kind, hence have some special explaining to do. And this explaining often involves an advocacy of the very ideas and conditions that made the explanation necessary in the first place.

One of the oldest doctrines of specialist-poets is that of the primacy of language and the primacy of poetry. They have virtually made a religion of their art, a religion based not on what they have in common with other people, but on what they *do* that sets them apart. For poets who believe this way, a poem is not a point of clarification or connection between themselves and the world on the one hand and between themselves and their readers on the other, nor is it an adventure into any reality or mystery outside themselves. It is a seeking of self in words, the making of a word-world in which the word-self may be at home. The poets go to their poems as other people have gone to the world or to God— for a sense of their own reality. Louis Simpson, for instance, says to an interviewer: "I have a very funny sense of myself in the poem—I'm not talking about me, I'm talking about how the poems make a self for me." Later he says of himself and some of his contemporaries: "We had to be devoted to poetry for its own sake."[1] And Mark Strand says: "I have the feeling that I am a metaphor for my own being."[2]

It may be argued, as Ransom does, that this emphasis was in some sense forced upon poets by their peculiar isolation in a society dominated by specialists of more practical kinds. But this way of looking at language and at poetry also completes and enforces the isolation of poets, not just within a sort of literary ghetto or subghetto, but within themselves. Mark Strand is evidently not the only poet who would say that "the self in a sense is all we have left."

This feeling is more particularly documented by Philip Levine, who anticipates, beyond the limits of his isolation, a reader—but an ideal reader with whom he may be in touch only by his poetry, with whom he will have no common ground except his poetry. Commenting on his assumption that he has no readers in his native city, he says to his interviewer: "I think it's terrific. I have a Detroit that vanished about 1952 for all I know, when I left. I live it, it's in my head, and it's got nothing to do with what's back there now." The world, then, is usable for poetry only after it has been totally subsumed in the self. Mr. Levine goes on to say of a visit to Spain: "By the end of the year the landscape seemed me, seemed like a projection of my own inner being. I felt that when I looked at the Spanish landscape I was looking at a part of myself."[3]

The world that once was mirrored by the poet has become the poet's mirror. This explains, I think, the emphasis upon personal terror and suffering and the fear of death in much recent poetry. When the self is one's exclusive subject and limit, reference and measure, one has no choice but to make a world of words. And this gives to one's own suffering and death the force of cataclysm.

But the difficulties are more than personal. For one thing, the subject of poetry is not words, it is the world, which poets have in common with other people. It has been argued that modern poets were forced to turn inward by the disposition of their materialistic societies to turn outward. But that argument ignores or discounts the traditions that have always bound poetry to the concerns and values of the spirit. This ancient allegiance gives poets the freedom, and perhaps the moral imperative, to turn outward. It is surely no accident that Yeats, perhaps the most spiritual poet in our language in our era, was also perhaps the most political. As regards this connection between humans and the world, the specialization of poetry is exactly analogous to the specialization of religion. Putting exclusive emphasis upon a world of words has the same result as putting exclusive emphasis upon heaven; it leads to, and allows, and abets the degradation of the world. And it leads ultimately to the degradation of poetry and religion. Renunciation of the world may sustain religious or poetic fervor for a while, but sooner or later it becomes suicidal.

This exclusive emphasis upon language leads also to the degradation of general literacy. Not so long ago it was generally thought that in order to be a writer a person needed extraordinary knowledge or experience. This, of course, frequently led to some willful absurdity in the life of a young writer. But it also suggested a connection—even a responsible connection—between art and experience or art and the world. What we have too frequently now, in the words of hundreds of poetry reviews in the time of my own coming of age, is the notion that what distinguishes a writer from a nonwriter is, first and last, a gift and a love of *language*. Writers, that is, are not distinguished by their knowledge or character or vision or inspiration or the stories they have to tell; they are distinguished by their specialties. This is a difference not of degree, but of kind. And the resulting absurdities are greater than before, and more dangerous. The power of such notions among the college-bred is suggested by a statement of Mr. John W. Dean III: "I would still like to be a writer. Maybe I will write a book. I love to play with words and twist phrases. I always play Scrabble."[4]

If both writer and reader assume that the writer's gift makes him or her a person of a radically different kind, then it seems that the relation between writer and reader must be radically reduced. Reading a book becomes merely a diversion. A writer such as Shakespeare is of course distinguished by his language, which is certainly his gift and his love. But his language is, after all, the common tongue, to which his gift is uncommon grace and power; without his commonness we could neither recognize nor value his distinction.

One of the first obligations of poets is certainly to purify the language of the tribe—but *not* merely to write poems with it. The language of the tribe used by a specialist-poet to produce a poem "for its own sake" can only describe the boundaries of an imprisoning and damning selfhood. Joyce Carol Oates says, writing of Sylvia Plath: "When the epic promise of 'One's-self I sing' is mistaken as the singing of a separate self, and not the Universal self, the results can only be tragic."[5] There is a sense of balance that is missing from the atmosphere that now surrounds much of the writing and much of the criticism of poetry. This sense of balance would lead and lead again to the poet's place of responsibility between the poem's readers and its subject—*which is also the readers' subject*. It would see words as fulcrums across which intelligence must endlessly be weighed against experience.

Another common ground is the literary tradition that joins all the sharers of literature, writers and readers, living and dead. But literary talk now seems remarkable for its lack of interest in tradition. The poets in the interviews are preoccupied with the new, with the modern world and modern times. They speak of very few poets who began to publish before World War II, almost none who lived before this century. Some of these poets seem to dismiss the past simply by lack of interest. Others show a sort of vindictiveness against it, typically expressed in generalized condemnations of traditional forms. Mark Strand says that "*we* [my emphasis] distrust rhyme because it sounds a little tinny, a little false, a little decorative, and a little unnatural. The point of writing . . . plain-style verse . . . is to affect as much as possible the naturalness of conversation, or plain discourse, not overly-excited discourse. Rhymes would get in the way. . . . I'm not talking about my own poetry when I say this. I'm sure Galway Kinnell and Robert Mezey . . . would not ever write in meters or rhyme." But Mr. Strand immediately confuses the issue by adding: "I've rhymed fairly recently, and I find it useful. I don't mind that, and I don't mind meters either. It sometimes seems quite natural to me."

Adrienne Rich apparently feels no such ambivalence. Her interviewer says: "Not many people anymore, not many poets anymore, talk very much, or feel they need to talk much, about form. Right?" And Rich replies: "Right! Or think very much about it." She calls Yeats "that table-rapping fascist," and says of her inability "to use the literature of the past": "I can't . . . read a poem by Yeats and feel somebody is talking to me whose voice I need to hear."[6]

William Matthews falls into line on the issue of traditional form, but his remarks on the subject are more elaborate and may afford some insight into the apparently widespread bias against form, traditional and otherwise. He believes, he says, "that one of the functions of art should be to disarrange patterns of certainty in the psyche. . . ." This century has produced "a life that is organized all too well, and . . . we really need to have our certainties shaken up badly." He says that it has never occurred to him to write in traditional forms because "I'm so much a believer in the notion of surprising yourself, and taking risks and preferring disorder to order, that it would be almost temperamentally impossible for me to do it."[7]

There are at least four false assumptions here: (1) that all "patterns of certainty" are false; (2) that there is no form except "traditional form"; (3) that the employment or the pursuit of form can lead only to what has been predetermined; (4) that organization is necessarily synonymous with order. The first of these assumptions may be simply an inadvertence of casual conversation: perhaps he meant "*false* patterns of certainty." To the first of these assumptions it can of course be said that, though the interest in form may be traditional, it is certainly possible to invent or to discover forms that are not traditional. The third assumption, it seems to me, is based on a misunderstanding of the nature and use of poetic form. The fourth assumption—of the identity of organization and order—is the most serious, because it fails to see the overwhelming disorder inherent in much, perhaps in most, twentieth-century organization.

The fear of chaos, Mr. Matthews maintains, originates with "people who get up every morning at eight o'clock, teach an Aesthetic Theory class at 10, get the department mail at twelve o'clock, give a graduate student exam in the afternoon, go home and have two drinks before dinner." Maybe so. But it seems to me more likely that the *praise* of chaos must come from people whose lives are so safely organized. Mr. Matthews does concede that "There's a kind of chaos which is awful—the moment before civilizations collapse, or when three members of your immediate family or friends are killed." But I do not believe that people who have experienced chaos are apt to praise or advocate any degree or variety of it. And to make these distinctions of value between kinds and degrees of chaos is both fanciful and dangerous. Formlessness is, after all, neither civilized nor natural. It is a peculiarly human evil, without analogue in nature, caused by the failures of civilization: inattention, irresponsibility, carelessness, ignorance of consequence. It is the result of the misuse of power. It is neither house nor field nor forest, but rather a war or a strip mine, where the balance between stability and change has been overthrown. The reason we need to have our *false* certainties shaken is so that we may see the possibility of better orders than we have.

Behind these and other perfunctory dismissals of traditional form there seems to be a feeling that these forms are not "organic." But I wonder if the distinction between organic and traditional is not misleading. A better set of terms, I think, would be organic and mechanical. There are some sonnets, for instance, whose form is organic; others whose form is mechanical. The difference apparently lies in the nature of the poem's conception and in the appropriateness or expressiveness of the form. And I do not see why a traditional verse form might not belong with complete propriety to what Denise Levertov calls the "constellation" of the experiences that make a poem.[8]

It may be necessary to question how much importance poets assign to statements they make to interviewers. But that Mr. Strand and Ms. Rich and Mr. Matthews spoke so casually and so generally of tradition and form, knowing that they spoke for publication, seems to imply an assumption that they spoke for many of their contemporaries. And though I am not sure how these statements are meant, they *sound* compulsively fashionable; they appear to have that eagerness to be up-to-date that identifies the modern cult of originality. That this eagerness to replace the old with the new justifies itself by the alleged uniqueness of the strains and demands of the modern world does not necessarily ennoble it: the modern world is after all largely the product of merchandisers, whose argument has been essentially the same.

Contemporaneity, in the sense of being "up with the times," is of no value. Wakefulness to experience—as well as to instruction and example—is another matter. But what we call the modern world is not necessarily, and not often, the real world, and there is no virtue in being up-to-date in it. It is a false world, based upon economies and values and desires that are fantastical—a world in which millions of people have lost any idea of the materials, the disciplines, the restraints, and the work necessary to support human life, and have thus become dangerous to their own lives and to the possibility of life. The job now is to get back to that perennial and substantial world in which we really do live, in which the foundations of our life will be visible to us, and in which we can accept our responsibilities again within the conditions of necessity and mystery. In that world all wakeful and responsible people, dead, living, and unborn, are contemporaries. And that is the only contemporaneity worth having.

What is needed is work of durable value; the time or age of it matters only after the value has been established. That a good poet is our contemporary reassures us of the continuing liveliness of certain possibilities; the contemporaneity of a worthless poet is a depressant. But there is much that we need that we cannot get from our contemporaries—even assuming that the work we have from them is the best that is possible: they cannot give us the sense of the longevity of human experience, the sense of the practicable, of *proven* possibility, that we get from older writing. Our past is not merely something to depart from; it is to commune with, to speak with: "Day unto day uttereth speech, and night unto night showeth knowledge." Remove this sense of continuity, and we are left with the thoughtless present tense of machines. If we fail to see that we live in the same world that Homer lived in, then we not only misunderstand Homer; we misunderstand ourselves. The past is our definition. We may strive, with good reason, to escape it, or to escape what is bad in it, but we will escape it only by adding something better to it.

If, as I believe, one of the functions of tradition is to convey a sense of our perennial nature and of the necessities and values that are the foundation of our life, then it follows that, without a live tradition, we are necessarily the prey of fashion: we have no choice but to emulate in the arts the "practical men" of commerce and industry whose mode of life is distraction of spirit and whose livelihood is the outdating of fads.

Isolated by the specialization of their art—by their tendency to make a religion of poetry or to make a world out of words, and by their preoccupation with the present and the new—poets of modern times seem to run extreme occupational risks. James Dickey says: "I think there is a terrible danger in the overcultivation of one's sensibilities, and that's what poets are forced to do in order to become poets." And: "In order to create poetry, you make a monster out of your own mind." He explains that some poets use alcohol or other drugs, first to coax the monster, and then to protect themselves from it. He mentions, as victims, John Berryman, Hart Crane, and Dylan Thomas, and calls poetry one of the most dangerous occupations in the world. But he believes that most of the victims have been content with their bargain: "Because the moments of intensity which do lead to delight and joy and fulfillment are so much better than those that other people have."⁹

The word "monster" is used in a perhaps similar way in the 285th of Berryman's *Dream Songs*. The poem speaks of Henry's struggling and darkness and confusion, and then says that "he took in his stride / more than most monsters can." It ends:

> Henry peered quite alone
> as if the worlds would answer to a code
> just around the corner, down gelid dawn,
> beckoning like a moan.

I think Mr. Dickey's mention of the use of drugs may give too limited a definition to the danger he is talking about, for associated with the possibility of a dependence on a drug is the possibility of a dependence on pain, a symbiosis in which a poet's work feeds on a suffering which, in turn, the work elaborates and augments, and again feeds on.

What I mainly want to question in Mr. Dickey's statement is the assumption that this monstrousness of mind and this suffering are necessary to the writing of poetry. There is no denying that poetry *can* be produced in this way—at least for a while. History certainly offers examples of unhappy or obsessed or mad poets, but it offers more examples of poets who sang or wrote in the exuberance of sanity, health, wholeness of spirit. One instantly credits Anne Sexton's statement that "Pain engraves a deeper memory,"¹⁰ not because one believes that it invariably does, but because one senses, in the modesty and brevity of the sentence, the probability that it *sometimes* does. But one can only be suspicious of the conclusion of the "afterthought" of Robert Lowell's *Notebook*: "In truth I seem to have felt mostly the joys of living; in remembering, in recording, thanks to the gift of the Muse, it is the pain."¹¹ One is simply aware of too much joyous poetry that has been the gift of the Muse, who apparently leaves the ratio of pain and joy to be determined by the poet. To attribute to the Muse a special fondness for pain is to come too close to desiring and cultivating pain. There is, I believe, some currency to the assumption that a fragmented, diseased people can make a whole and healthy art out of their fragmentation and disease. It has not yet been done. Yeats says that "neither scholars nor the populace have sung or read anything generation after generation because of its pain."[12]

The danger may not be so much in the overcultivation of sensibility as in its *exclusive* cultivation. Sensibility becomes the inescapable stock in trade of the isolated poet, who is increasingly cut off from both song and story because the nature of these is communal. And isolation, or the sense of isolation, is moving much of our poetry toward the tone, rhythm, and structure of what Mark Strand calls "not overly excited discourse." This is what Denise Levertov calls "an unexampled production of *notations*: poems which tell of things seen or done, but . . . do not impart a sense of the experiencing of seeing or doing, or of the *value* of such experience. . . ." And she says that "The lack of a unifying intelligence, of the implicit presence of an interpreting spirit behind the notation, is associated—and not accidentally—with a lack of music."[13] The union of overcultivated sensibility and undercultivated verse cannot produce song. It produces—not prose—but the prosaic, unessential prose. The art does not press hard enough against experience.

I find it impossible to believe that song can come from, or lead to, isolation. If a poet says, "I vnto my selfe alone will sing," as Spenser does at the beginning of his "Epithalamion," he can only mean that he does so in anticipation of accompaniment or at least of company. A poet who felt assured that he sang to himself alone would soon find his song lapsing diffidently into a "not overly excited discourse" on the subject of isolation, guilt, suffering, death, and oblivion—the self-exploiting autobiography of disconnected sensibility.

Song is natural; we have it in common with animals. For humans, it is also artificial and traditional; it has to be made by someone who knows how to make it and sung *to* someone who will recognize it as song. Rhythm, fundamental to it, is its profoundest *reference*. The rhythm of a song or a poem rises, no doubt, in reference to the pulse and breath of the poet, as is often repeated, but that is still too specialized an accounting; it rises also in reference to daily and seasonal—and surely even longer—rhythms in the life of the poet and in the life that surrounds him. The rhythm of a poem resonates with these larger rhythms that surround it; it fills its environment with sympathetic vibrations. Rhyme, which is a function of rhythm, may suggest this sort of resonance; it marks the coincidences of smaller structures with larger ones, as when the day, the month, and the year all end at the same moment. Song, then, is a force opposed to specialty and to isolation. It is the testimony of the singer's inescapable relation to the world, to the human community, and also to tradition.

But even more suggestive of the specialization of contemporary poets is their estrangement from storytelling. Typically, one can find this debility cited as a virtue and a goal. In an interview that is in general far more carefully spoken and better considered than most, Galway Kinnell says: "I would like a poem to be able to be free of narrative." One needs to know the reasons that lie behind this statement, but the interview does not produce them. Mr. Kinnell says only that "If a poem could be free of narrative altogether, it would at least open the possibility that some truth could be said directly rather than by parable."[14] But he is never asked the two obvious questions: how this might be possible, and why it might be desirable.

(I must acknowledge a certain unfairness, here as earlier, in challenging a poet's statement in the absence of his argument. I assume, however, that the general absence, in these interviews, of the questions that would have produced the arguments must imply either that the statements are all so widely credited that there is no apparent need to explain or support them, or that specialization imposes an ethic or etiquette that automatically concedes the virtue of anything whatever that a poet says about poetry.)

Though I believe that freedom from narrative has not often been advocated as a goal, there can be no question that the narrative power of poetry has been in decline for generations, until it is now little more than inadvertent. Our century has produced several poems that poets and readers have called "epic," but both character and story, in the old senses of the terms, are absent from most. ("Epic," as the word is now often used, seems to mean little more than major or ambitious or long.) That so accomplished a poet as Galway Kinnell now speaks of the suppression of narrative as a goal is, it seems to me, a serious matter, especially as it is only the latest in a series of programs to renew or purify poetry by reducing its means. Why is it necessary for poets to believe, like salesmen, that the new inevitably must replace or destroy the old? Why cannot poetry renew itself and advance into new circumstance by *adding* the new to the old? Why cannot the critical faculty, in poets and critics alike, undertake to see that *the best* of the new is grafted to *the best* of the old? Free verse, for instance, is a diminishment of the competence of poetry if it is seen as *replacing* traditional prosody; it is an enlargement only if it is conceived as an addition. Freedom from narrative is a diminishment—it is not even a freedom—unless it is included with the capability of narrative among the live possibilities of poetry. To attempt to advance by more taking away is not to bring into view a renewed and newly powerful art. It heads us instead toward what Mr. Kinnell himself warns against: "the other possibility, that to exist at all poetry will simply give up its old ambitions and adapt itself to what is, that it will simply become the expression of a reality from which all trace of the sacred has been removed."

But this weakening of narrative in poetry—whether by policy, indifference, or debility—may be one of the keys to what is wrong with us, both as poets and as people. It is indicative of a serious lack of interest, first, in action, and second, in *responsible* action. Muir said that "the story, although it is our story, is disappearing from poetry." And he said: "The old story . . . followed some figure—Odysseus, or Ruth, or King David— through time; and it remains the most pure image that we have of temporal life, tracing the journey which we shall take." Narrative poetry records, contemplates, hands down the actions of the past. Poetry has a responsibility to remember and to preserve and reveal the truth about these actions. But it also has a complementary responsibility that is equally public: to help to preserve and to clarify the possibility of *responsible* action. Ezra Pound, perhaps more than anyone else in our time, insisted on this as the social value of "the damned and despised *litterati*:" "When their work goes rotten . . . when their very medium, the very essence of their work, the application of word to thing goes rotten, i.e. becomes slushy and inexact, or excessive or bloated, the whole machinery of social and of individual thought and order goes to pot."[15] The word "order," as used here, clearly refers to the possibility of responsible action, the possibility of good work.

But our malaise, both in our art and in our lives, is that we have lost sight of the possibility of right or responsible action. Publicly, we have delegated our capacity to act to men who are capable of action only because they cannot think. Privately, as in much of our poetry, we communicate by ironic or cynical *allusions* to that debased tale of futility, victimization, and defeat, which we seem to have elected to be our story. The prevailing tendency, in poetry and out, is to see people not as actors, but as sufferers. What are John Berryman's dream songs, brilliant as they sometimes are, but the mortifications of a splendid intelligence helpless before its salient occasions? To how great an extent is modern poetry the record of highly refined sensibilities that could think or feel but not do? And must not this passiveness of the poetic sensibility *force* its withdrawal into the world of words where, for want of the sustenance of action, it becomes despondent and self-destructive? "Poems," wrote Randall Jarrell's widow, "flew at him . . . until just words beat at his head like many wings."[16]

In the last ten years there has been a reaction against this passivity. But for the most part this has produced only protest, which is either a gesture and not an action at all, or a negative action that either repudiates or opposes. The shallowness of protest is in this negativity; it is also in the short-winded righteousness by which it condemns evils for which it accepts no responsibility. In itself, protest implies no discipline and no correction. "A public man," Edwin Muir wrote, "is a man who is entitled to be listened to by the public; a great public man is one who can tell his public on occasion, what he thinks of them, knowing that they will listen. This was the position which Yeats achieved, alone among the poets of his time." That we have no poets who are, in that sense, public persons suggests even more forcibly the weakness of our poetry of protest. In his protest, the contemporary poet is speaking publicly, but not as a spokesman; he is only one outraged citizen speaking *at* other citizens who do not know him, whom he does not know, and with whom he does not sympathize. The tone of self-righteousness is one result of this circumstance.

In "Poets without Laurels," Ransom holds that the specialization of poetry was "inevitable" because of the specialization of the age, though he ventures to say that "the modern program, on the whole, is not the one under which men maintain their best health and spirits." Muir, on the other hand, does not look upon the alienation of poets from their audience as inevitable. *The Estate of Poetry* is remarkable for the practicality of its purpose; it faces up to the social and historical context of the problem, and then it argues toward a solution: "Public indifference may be expected to continue, but perhaps the audience will increase when poetry loses what obscurity is left in it by attempting greater themes, for great themes have to be treated clearly. A great theme greatly treated might still put poetry back in its old place." And at the end of his book Muir wrote: "There remains the temptation for poets to turn inward into poetry, to lock themselves into a hygienic prison where they speak only to one another, and to the critic. . . . In the end a poet must create his audience and to do that he must turn outward."

It may be that poets can make this outward turn and regain the great themes only by taking up again their old interest in action—by renewing the knowledge and meaning of actions known from the past and by considering the possibility of *right* action now and in the future. Perhaps they will have to repudiate those purely negative actions by which we dissociate ourselves from other people. It is certain that there are better actions. There are actions worthy of the patience and work of whole lives—actions, even, that no whole life can complete—that involve the lives of people in the lives of places and communities. Without such actions, both in life and in art, the consciousness of our people will be fragmentary. How can we explain what Berryman called "the mysterious late excellence" of William Carlos Williams, if not by his community life as a doctor, that carried his art again and again to the test and the renewal of acts? And must not the late excellence of Yeats have been indebted to his passionate involvement in the fate of Ireland?

It would be ungrateful and stupid to condemn and turn our backs on the work of inward-turned poets. That work contains much of value that we need to cherish and to learn from. It is only necessary to understand that that work has flourished upon, and has fostered, a grievous division between life and work, as have the other specialized disciplines of our era, and that that division has made it possible for work to turn upon and exploit and destroy life.

Perhaps the time has come to say that there is, in reality, no such choice as Yeats's "Perfection of the life, or of the work." The division implied by this proposed choice is not only destructive; it is based upon a shallow understanding of the relation between work and life. The conflicts of life and work, like those of rest and work, would ideally be resolved in balance: *enough* of each. In practice, however, they probably can be resolved (if that is the word) only in tension, in a principled unwillingness to let go of either, or to sacrifice either to the other. But it is a *necessary* tension, the grief in it both inescapable and necessary. One would like, one longs in fact, to be perfect family man *and* a perfect workman. And one suffers from the inevitable conflicts. But whatever one does, one is not going to be perfect at either, and it is better to suffer the imperfection of both than to gamble the total failure of one against an illusory hope of perfection in the other. The real values of art and life are perhaps best defined and felt in the tension between them. The effort to perfect work rises out of, and communes with and in turn informs, the effort to perfect life, as Yeats himself knew and as other poems of his testify. The *use* of life to perfect work is an evil of the specialized intellect. It makes of the most humane of disciplines an exploitive industry.

NOTES

1. *The Ohio Review*, Spring 1973.
2. *The Ohio Review*, Winter 1972.
3. *American Poetry Review*, November–December 1972.
4. Mary McGrory, "The Dean Story," in the *Louisville Courier-Journal*, May 16, 1973.
5. *The Southern Review*, Summer 1973.
6. *The Ohio Review*, Fall 1971.
7. *The Ohio Review*, Spring 1972.
8. "Some Notes on Organic Form," *The Poet in the World*.
9. *Playboy*, November 1973.
10. *The Paris Review*, Number 52.
11. Third edition, 1970.
12. "A General Introduction for My Work," *Essays and Introductions*.
13. "Great Possessions," *The Poet in the World*.
14. *The Ohio Review*, Fall 1972.

15. "How to Read," *Literary Essays of Ezra Pound.*
16. "The Group of Two" in Lowell, et al, *Randall Jarrell 1914–1965.*

2 Standing by Words (1979)

"He said, and stood . . ."
Paradise Regained, IV, 561.

Two epidemic illnesses of our time—upon both of which virtual industries of cures have been founded—are the disintegration of communities and the disintegration of persons. That these two are related (that private loneliness, for instance, will necessarily accompany public confusion) is clear enough. And I take for granted that most people have explored in themselves and their surroundings some of the intricacies of the practical causes and effects; most of us, for example, have understood that the results are usually bad when people act in social or moral isolation, and also when, because of such isolation, they fail to act.

What seems not so well understood, because not so much examined, is the relation between these disintegrations and the disintegration of language. My impression is that we have seen, for perhaps a hundred and fifty years, a gradual increase in language that is either meaningless or destructive of meaning. And I believe that this increasing unreliability of language parallels the increasing disintegration, over the same period, of persons and communities.

My concern is for the *accountability* of language—hence, for the accountability of the users of language. To deal with this matter I will use a pair of economic concepts: *internal account-ing*, which considers costs and benefits in reference only to the interest of the money-making enterprise itself; and *external ac-counting*, which considers the costs and benefits to the "larger community." By altering the application of these terms a little, any statement may be said to account well or poorly for what is going on inside the speaker, or outside him, or both.

It will be found, I believe, that the accounting will be poor—incomprehensible or unreliable—if it attempts to be purely in-ternal or purely external. One of the primary obligations of lan-guage is to connect and balance the two kinds of accounting.

And so, in trying to understand the degeneracy of language, it is necessary to examine, not one kind of unaccountability, but two complementary kinds. There is language that is diminished by subjectivity, which ends in meaninglessness. But that kind of language rarely exists alone (or so I believe), but is accompanied, in a complex relationship of both cause and effect, by a language diminished by objectivity, or so-called objectivity (inordinate or irresponsible ambition), which ends in confusion.

My standpoint here is defined by the assumption that no state-ment is complete or comprehensible in itself, that in order for a statement to be complete and comprehensible three conditions are required:

1. It must designate its object precisely.

2. Its speaker must stand by it: must believe it, be accountable for it, be willing to act on it.

3. This relation of speaker, word, and object must be conven-tional; the community must know what it is.

These are still the common assumptions of private conversa-tions. In our ordinary dealings with each other, we take for granted that we cannot understand what is said if we cannot as-sume the accountability of the speaker, the accuracy of his speech, and mutual agreement on the structures of language and the meanings of words. We assume, in short, that language is communal, and that its purpose is to tell the truth.

That these common assumptions are becoming increasingly uncommon, particularly in the discourse of specialists of various sorts, is readily evident to anyone looking for evidence. How far they have passed from favor among specialists of language, to use the handiest example, is probably implicit in the existence of such specialists; one could hardly become a language specialist (a "scientist" of language) so long as one adhered to the old assumptions.

But the influence of these specialists is, of course, not confined to the boundaries of their specializations. They write textbooks for people who are not specialists of language, but who are apt to become specialists of other kinds. The general purpose of at least some of these specialists, and its conformability to the purposes of specialists of other kinds, is readily suggested by a couple of recently published textbooks for freshman English.

One of these, *The Contemporary Writer*, by W. Ross Winterowd,[1] contains a chapter on language, the main purpose of which is to convince the student of the illegitimate tyranny of any kind of prescriptive grammar and of the absurdity of judging language "on the basis of extra-linguistic considerations." This chapter proposes four rules that completely overturn all the old common assumptions:

1. "Languages apparently do not become better or worse in any sense. They simply change."

2. "Language is arbitrary."

3. "Rightness and wrongness are determined . . . by the purpose for which the language is being used, by the audience at which it is directed, and by the situation in which the use is taking place."

4. ". . . a grammar of a language is a description of that language, nothing more and nothing less."

And these rules have a pair of corollaries that Mr. Winterowd states plainly. One is that "you [the freshman student] have a more or less complete mastery of the English language. . . ." The other is that art—specifically, here, the literary art—is "the highest expression of the human need to play, of the desire to escape from the world of reality into the world of fantasy."

The second of these texts, *Rhetoric: Discovery and Change*, by Richard E. Young, Alton L. Becker, and Kenneth L. Pike,[2] takes the standardless functionalism of Mr. Winterowd's understanding of language and applies it to the use of language. "The ethical dimension of the art of rhetoric," these authors say, is in "the attempt to reduce another's sense of threat in the effort to reach the goal of cooperation and mutual benefit. . . ." They distinguish between evaluative writing and descriptive writing, preferring the latter because evaluative writing tends to cause people "to become defensive," whereas "a description . . . does not make judgments. . . ." When, however, a writer "must make judgments, he can make them in a way that minimizes the reader's sense of threat." Among other things, "he can acknowledge the personal element in his judgment. . . . There is a subtle but important difference between saying 'I don't like it' and 'It's bad.' "

The authors equate evaluation—functionally, at least—with dogmatism: "The problem with dogmatism is that, like evaluation, it forces the reader to take sides." And finally they recommend a variety of writing which they call "provisional" because it "focuses on the process of enquiry itself and acknowledges the tentative nature of conclusions. . . . Provisional writing implies that more than one reasonable conclusion is possible."

The first of these books attempts to make the study of language an "objective" science by eliminating from that study all extra-linguistic values and the issue of quality. Mr. Winterowd asserts that "the language grows according to its own dynamics." He does not say, apparently because he does not believe, that its dynamics include the influence of the best practice. There is no "best." Anyone who speaks English is a "master" of the language. And the writers once acknowledged as masters of English are removed from "the world of reality" to the "world of fantasy," where they lose their force within the dynamics of the growth of language. Their works are reduced to the feckless status of "experiences": "we are much more interested in the imaginative statement of the message . . . than we are in the message. . . ." Mr. Winterowd's linguistic "science" thus views language as an organism that has evolved without reference to habitat. Its growth has been "arbitrary," without any principle of selectivity.

Against Mr. Winterowd's definition of literature, it will be instructive to place a definition by Gary Snyder, who says of poetry that it is "a tool, a net or trap to catch and present; a sharp edge; a medicine, or the little awl that unties knots."[3] It will be quickly observed that this sentence enormously complicates Mr. Winterowd's simplistic statement-message dichotomy. What Mr. Winterowd means by "message" is an "idea" written in the dullest possible prose. His book is glib, and glibness is an inescapable doom of language without standards. One of the great practical uses of literary disciplines, of course, is to resist glibness—to slow language down and make it thoughtful. This accounts for the influence of verse, in its formal aspect, within the dynamics of the growth of language: verse checks the merely impulsive flow of speech, subjects it to another pulse, to measure, to extra-linguistic considerations; by inducing the hesitations of difficulty, it admits into language the influence of the Muse and of musing.

The three authors of the second book attempt to found an ethics of rhetoric on the idea expressed in one of Mr. Winterowd's rules: "Rightness and wrongness are determined" by purpose, audience, and situation. This idea apparently derives from, though it significantly reduces, the ancient artistic concern for propriety or decorum. A part of this concern was indeed the fittingness of the work to its occasion: that is, one would not write an elegy in the meter of a drinking song—though that is putting it too plainly, for the sense of occasion exercised an influence both broad and subtle on form, diction, syntax, small points of grammar and prosody—everything. But occasion, as I understand it, was invariably second in importance to the subject. It is only the modern specialist who departs from this. The specialist poet, for instance, degrades the subject to "subject matter" or raw material, so that the subject exists for the poem's sake, is *subjected* to the poem, in the same way as industrial specialists see trees or ore-bearing rocks as raw material subjected to their manufactured end-products. Quantity thus begins to dominate the work of the specialist poet at its source. Like an industrialist, he is interested in the subjects of the world for the sake of what they can be made to produce. He mines his experience for subject matter. The first aim of the propriety of the old poets, by contrast, was to make the language true to its subject—to see that it told the truth. That is why they invoked the Muse. The truth the poet chose as his subject was perceived as *superior* to his powers—and, by clear implication, to his occasion and purpose. But the aim of truth-telling is not stated in either of these textbooks. The second, in fact, makes an "ethical" aim of avoiding the issue, for, as the authors say, coining a formidable truth: "Truth has become increasingly elusive and men are driven to embrace conflicting ideologies."

This sort of talk about language, it seems to me, is fundamentally impractical. It does not propose as an outcome any fidelity between words and speakers or words and things or words and acts. It leads instead to muteness and paralysis. So far as I can tell, it is unlikely that one could speak at all, in even the most casual conversation, without some informing sense of what would be best to say—that is, without some sort of *standard*. And I do not believe that it is possible to act on the basis of a "tentative" or "provisional" conclusion. We may know that we are forming a conclusion on the basis of provisional or insufficient knowledge—that is a part of what we understand as the tragedy of our condition. But we must act, nevertheless, on the basis of *final* conclusions, because we know that actions, occurring in time, are irrevocable. That is another part of our tragedy. People who make a conventional agreement that all conclusions are provisional—a convention almost invariably implied by academic uses of the word "objectivity"—characteristically talk but do not act. Or they do not act deliberately, though time and materiality carry them into action of a sort, willy-nilly.

And there are times, according to the only reliable ethics we have, when one is required to tell the truth, whatever the urgings of purpose, audience, and situation. Ethics requires this because, in the terms of the practical realities of our lives, the truth is safer than falsehood. To ignore this is simply to put language at the service of purpose—*any* purpose. It is, in terms of the most urgent realities of our own time, to abet a dangerous confusion between public responsibility and public relations. Remote as these theories of language are from practical contexts, they are nevertheless serviceable to expedient practices.

In affirming that there is a necessary and indispensable connection between language and truth, and therefore between language and deeds, I have certain precedents in mind. I begin with the Christian idea of the Incarnate Word, the Word entering the world as flesh, and inevitably therefore as action—which leads logically enough to the insistence in the Epistle of James that faith without works is dead:

> For if any be a hearer of the word, and not a doer, he is like unto a man beholding his natural face in a glass:
> For he beholdeth himself, and goeth his way, and straightway forgetteth what manner of man he was.[4]

I also have in mind the Confucian insistence on sincerity (precision) and on fidelity between speaker and word as essentials of political health: "Honesty is the treasure of states." I have returned to Ezra Pound's observation that Confucius "collected *The Odes* to keep his followers from abstract discussion. That is, *The Odes* give particular instances. They do not lead to exaggerations of dogma."[5]

And I have remembered from somewhere Thoreau's sentence: "Where would you look for standard English but to the words of a standard man?"

The idea of standing by one's word, of words precisely designating things, of deeds faithful to words, is probably native to our understanding. Indeed, it seems doubtful that we could understand anything without that idea.

But in order to discover what makes language that can be understood, stood by, and acted on, it is necessary to return to my borrowed concepts of internal and external accounting. And it will be useful to add two further precedents.

In *Mind and Nature*, Gregory Bateson writes that " 'things' . . . can only enter the world of communication and meaning by their names, their qualities and their attributes (i.e., by reports of their internal and external relations and interactions)."[6]

And Gary Snyder, in a remarkably practical or practicable or practice-able definition of where he takes his stand, makes the poet responsible for "possibilities opening both inward and outward."[7]

There can be little doubt, I think, that any accounting that is *purely* internal will be incomprehensible. If the connection between inward and outward is broken—if, for instance, the experience of a single human does not resonate within the common experience of humanity—then language fails. In *The Family Reunion*, Harry says: "I talk in general terms / Because the particular has no language."[8] But he speaks, too, in despair, having no hope that his general terms can communicate the particular burden of his experience. We readily identify this loneliness of personal experience as "modern." Many poems of our century have this loneliness, this failure of speech, as a subject; many more exhibit it as a symptom.

But it begins at least as far back as Shelley, in such lines as these from "Stanzas Written in Dejection, Near Naples":

Alas! I have nor hope nor health,
    Nor peace within nor calm around,
Nor that content surpassing wealth

> The sage in meditation found,
>   And walked with inward glory crowned—
> Nor fame, nor power, nor love, nor leisure.
>
> ....
>
> I could lie down like a tired child,
>   And weep away the life of care
>   Which I have borne and must bear,
> Till death like sleep might steal on me . . .

This too is an example of particular experience concealing itself in "general terms"—though here the failure, if it was suspected, is not acknowledged. The generality of the language does not objectify it, but seals it in its subjectivity. In reading this—as, I think, in reading a great many poems of our own time—we sooner or later realize that we are reading a "complaint" that we do not credit or understand. If we fail to realize this, it is because we have departed from the text of the poem, summoning particularities of our own experience in support of Shelley's general assertions. The fact remains that Shelley's poem doesn't tell us what he is complaining about; his lines fail to "create the object [here, the experience] which they contemplate."[9] The poem has forsaken its story. This failure is implicitly conceded by the editors of *The Norton Anthology of English Literature*, who felt it necessary to provide the following footnote:

> Shelley's first wife, Harriet, had drowned herself; Clara, his baby daughter by Mary Shelley, had just died; and Shelley himself was plagued by ill health, pain, financial worries, and the sense that he had failed as a poet.[10]

But I think the poem itself calls attention to the failure by its easy descent into self-pity, finally asserting that "I am one / Whom men love not. . . ." Language that becomes too subjective lacks currency, to use another economic metaphor; it will not pass. Self-pity, like self-praise, will not pass. The powers of language are used illegitimately, to impose, rather than to elicit, the desired response.

Shelley is not writing gibberish here. It is possible to imagine that someone who does not dislike this poem may see in it a certain beauty. But it is the sickly beauty of generalized emotionalism. For once precision is abandoned as a linguistic or literary virtue, vague generalization is one of the two remaining possibilities, gibberish being the second. And without precise accounting, leading to responsible action, there is no escape from the Shelleyan rhythm of exaltation and despair—ideal passions culminating in real disasters.

It is true, in a sense, that "the particular has no language"—that at least in public writing, and in speech passing between strangers, there may only be degrees of generalization. But there are, I think, two kinds of precision that are particular and particularizing. There is, first, the precision in the speech of people who share the same knowledge of place and history and work. This is the precision of direct reference or designation. It sounds like this: "How about letting me borrow your tall jack?" Or: "The old hollow beech blew down last night." Or, beginning a story, "Do you remember that time . . . ?" I would call this community speech. Its words have the power of pointing to things visible either to eyesight or to memory. Where it is not much corrupted by public or media speech, this community speech is wonderfully vital. Because it so often works designatively it *has* to be precise, and its precisions are formed by persistent testing against its objects.

This community speech, unconsciously taught and learned, in which words live in the presence of their objects, is the very root and foundation of language. It is the source, the unconscious inheritance that is carried, both with and without schooling, into consciousness—but never *all* the way, and so it remains rich, mysterious, and enlivening. Cut off from this source, language becomes a paltry work of conscious purpose, at the service and the mercy of expedient aims. Theories such as those underlying the two textbooks I have discussed seem to be attempts to detach language from its source in communal experience, by

making it arbitrary in origin and provisional in use. And this
may be a "realistic" way of "accepting" the degradation of community life. The task, I think, is hopeless, and it shows the extremes of futility that academic specialization can lead to. If one
wishes to promote the life of language, one must promote the life
of the community—a discipline many times more trying, difficult, and long than that of linguistics, but having at least the virtue of hopefulness. It escapes the despair always implicit in specializations: the cultivation of discrete parts without respect or
responsibility for the whole.

The other sort of precision—the sort available to public speech
or writing as well as to community speech—is a precision that
comes of tension either between a statement and a prepared context or, within a single statement, between more or less conflicting feelings or ideas. Shelley's complaint is incomprehensible
not just because it is set in "general terms," but because the generalities are too simple. One doesn't credit the emotion of the
poem because it is too purely mournful. We are—conventionally, maybe, but also properly—unprepared to believe without
overpowering evidence that things are *all* bad. Self-pity may deal
in such absolutes of feeling, but we don't deal with other people
in the manner of self-pity.

Another general complaint about mortality is given in Act V,
Scene 2, of *King Lear*, when Edgar says to Gloucester: "Men
must endure / Their going hence, even as their coming hither."
Out of context this statement is even more general than Shelley's. It is, unlike Shelley's, deeply moving because it is tensely
poised within a narrative context that makes it precise. We know
exactly, for instance, what is meant by that "must": a responsible performance is required until death. But the complaint is followed immediately by a statement of another kind, forcing the
speech of the play back into its action: "Ripeness is all. Come
on."

Almost the same thing is done in a single line of Robert Herrick, in the tension between the complaint of mortality and the jaunty metric:

> Out of the world he must, who once comes in . . .

Here the very statement of inevitable death sings its acceptability. How would you divide, there, the "statement of the message" from "the message"?

And see how the tension between contradictory thoughts particularizes the feeling in these three lines by John Dryden:

> Old as I am, for Ladies Love unfit,
> The Pow'r of Beauty I remember yet,
> Which once inflam'd my Soul, and still inspires my Wit.

These last three examples immediately receive our belief and sympathy because they satisfy our sense of the complexity, the cross-graining, of real experience. In them, an inward possibility is made to open outward. Internal accounting has made itself externally accountable.

Shelley's poem, on the other hand, exemplifies the solitude of inward experience that continues with us, both in and out of poetry. I don't pretend to understand all the causes and effects of this, but I will offer the opinion that one of its chief causes is a simplistic idea of "freedom," which also continues with us, and is also to be found in Shelley. At the end of Act III of *Prometheus Unbound*, we are given this vision of a liberated humanity:

> The loathsome mask has fallen, the man remains
> Sceptreless, free, uncircumscribed, but man
> Equal, unclassed, tribeless, and nationless,
> Exempt from awe, worship, degree, the king
> Over himself . . .

This passage, like the one from the "Stanzas Written in Dejection," is vague enough, and for the same reason; as the first hastened to emotional absolutes, this hastens to an absolute idea. It is less a vision of a free man than a vision of a definition of a free man. But Shelley apparently did not notice that this headlong scramble of adjectives, though it may produce one of the possible definitions of a free man, also defines a lonely one, unattached and displaced. This free man is described as loving, and love is an emotion highly esteemed by Shelley. But it is, like his misery, a "free" emotion, detached and absolute. In this same passage of *Prometheus Unbound*, he calls it "the nepenthe, love"—love forgetful, or inducing forgetfulness, of grief or pain.

Shelley thought himself, particularly in *Prometheus Unbound*, a follower of Milton—an assumption based on a misunderstanding of *Paradise Lost*. And so it is instructive in two ways to set beside Shelley's definition of freedom this one by Milton:

> To be free is precisely the same thing as to be pious, wise, just, and temperate, careful of one's own, abstinent from what is another's, and thence, in fine, magnanimous and brave.[11]

And Milton's definition, like the lines previously quoted from Shakespeare, Herrick, and Dryden, derives its precision from tension: he defines freedom in terms of responsibilities. And it is only this tension that can suggest the possibility of *living* (for any length of time) in freedom—just as it is the tension between love and pain that suggests the possibility of carrying love into acts. Shelley's freedom, defined in terms of freedom, gives us only this from a "Chorus of Spirits" in Act IV, Scene 1, of *Prometheus Unbound*:

> Our task is done,
> We are free to dive, or soar, or run;
>   Beyond and around,
>   Or within the bound
> Which clips the world with darkness round.
>
>   We'll pass the eyes
>   Of the starry skies
> Into the hoar deep to colonize . . .

Which, as we will see, has more in common with the technological romanticism of Buckminster Fuller than with anything in Milton.

In supposed opposition to this remote subjectivity of internal accounting, our age has developed a stance or state of mind which it calls "objective," and which produces a kind of accounting supposed to be external—that is, free from personal biases and considerations. This objective mentality, within the safe confines of its various specialized disciplines, operates with great precision and confidence. It follows tested and trusted procedures and uses a professional language that an outsider must assume to be a very exact code. When this language is used by its accustomed speakers on their accustomed ground, even when one does not understand it, it clearly voices the implication of a marvelously precise control over objective reality. It is only when it is overheard in confrontation with failure that this implication falters, and the adequacy of this sort of language comes into doubt.

The transcribed conversations of the members of the Nuclear Regulatory Commission during the crisis of Three Mile Island[12] provide a valuable exhibit of the limitations of one of these objective languages. At one point, for example, the commissioners received a call from Roger Mattson, Nuclear Reactor Regulation chief of systems safety. He said, among other things, the following:

> That bubble will be 5,000 cubic feet. The available volume in the upper head and the candy canes, that's the hot legs, is on the order of 2,000 cubic feet total. I get 3,000 excess cubic feet of noncondensibles. I've got a horse race. . . . We have got every systems engineer we can find. . . thinking the problem: how the hell do we get the noncondensibles out of there, do we win the horse race or do we lose the horse race.

At another time the commissioners were working to "engineer a press release," of which "The focus . . . has to be reassuring. . . ." Commissioner Ahearne apparently felt that it was a bit *too* reassuring, and he would have liked to *suggest* the possibility of a bad outcome, apparently a meltdown. He said:

> I think it would be technically a lot better if you said—something about there's a possibility—it's small, but it could lead to serious problems.

And, a few sentences later, Commissioner Kennedy told him:

> Well I understand what you're saying. . . . You could put a little sentence in right there . . . to say, were this—in the unlikely event that this occurred, increased temperatures would result and possible further fuel damage.

What is remarkable, and frightening, about this language is its inability to admit what it is talking about. Because these specialists have routinely eliminated themselves, as such and as representative human beings, from consideration, according to the prescribed "objectivity" of their discipline, they cannot bring themselves to acknowledge to each other, much less to the public, that their problem involves an extreme danger to a lot of people. Their subject, as bearers of a public trust, is this danger, and it can be nothing else. It is a technical problem least of all. And yet when their language approaches this subject, it either diminishes it, or dissolves into confusions of both syntax and purpose. Mr. Mattson speaks clearly and coherently enough so long as numbers and the jargon of "candy canes" and "hot legs" are adequate to his purpose. But as soon as he tries to communicate his sense of the human urgency of the problem, his language collapses into a kind of rant around the metaphor of "a horse race," a metaphor that works, not to reveal, but to obscure his meaning. And the two commissioners, struggling with their obligation to inform the public of the possibility of a disaster, find themselves virtually languageless—without the necessary words and with only the shambles of a syntax. They cannot say what they are talking about. And so their obligation to *inform* becomes a tongue-tied—and therefore surely futile—effort to *re-*

assure. Public responsibility becomes public relations, apparently, for want of a language adequately responsive to its subject.

So inept is the speech of these commissioners that we must deliberately remind ourselves that they are not stupid and are probably not amoral. They are highly trained, intelligent, worried men, whose understanding of language is by now to a considerable extent a public one. They are atomic scientists whose criteria of language are identical to those of at least some linguistic scientists. They determine the correctness of their statement to the press exactly according to Mr. Winterowd's rule: by their purpose, audience, and situation. Their language is governed by the ethical aim prescribed by the three authors of *Rhetoric: Discovery and Change*: they wish above all to speak in such a way as to "reduce another's sense of threat." But the result was not "cooperation and mutual benefit"; it was incoherence and dishonesty, leading to public suspicion, distrust, and fear. It is beneficial, surely, to "reduce another's sense of threat" only if there is no threat.

The Commissioners speak a language that is diminished by inordinate ambition: the taking of more power than can be responsibly or beneficently held. It is perhaps a law of human nature that such ambition always produces a confusion of tongues:

> And they said, Go to, let us build us a city and a tower, whose top may reach unto heaven; and let us make us a name, lest we be scattered
>
> . . . .
>
> And the Lord said . . . now nothing will be restrained from them, which they have imagined to do.
>
> Go to, let us go down, and there confound their language, that they may not understand one another's speech.[13]

The professed aim is to bring people together—usually for the implicit, though unstated, purpose of subjecting them to some public power or project. Why else would rulers seek to "unify" people? The idea is to cause them to speak the same language—meaning either that they will agree with the government or be quiet, as in communist and fascist states, or that they will polite-

ly ignore their disagreements or disagree "provisionally," as in
American universities. But the result—though power may survive for a while in spite of it—is confusion and dispersal. Real
language, real discourse are destroyed. People lose understanding of each other, are divided and scattered. Speech of whatever
kind begins to resemble the speech of drunkenness or madness.

What this dialogue of the Nuclear Regulatory Commissioners causes one to suspect—and I believe the suspicion is confirmed by every other such exhibit I have seen—is that there is
simply no such thing as an accounting that is *purely* external.
The notion that external accounting can be accomplished by
"objectivity" is an illusion. Apparently the only way to free the
accounting of what is internal to people, or subjective, is to make
it internal to (that is subject to) some other entity or structure just
as limiting, or more so—as the commissioners attempted to deal
with a possible public catastrophe in terms either of nuclear
technology or of public relations. The only thing really externalized by such accounting is a bad result that one does not wish to
pay for.

And so external accounting, alone, is only another form of internal accounting. The only difference is that this "objective" accounting does pretty effectively rule out personal considerations
of a certain kind. (It does *not* rule out the personal desire for
wealth, power, or for intellectual certainty.) Otherwise, the talk
of the commissioners and the lines from "Stanzas Written in Dejection" are equally and similarly incomprehensible. The languages of both are obviously troubled, we recognize the words,
and learn something about the occasions, but we cannot learn
from the language itself exactly what the trouble is. The commissioners' language cannot define the problem of their public responsibility, and Shelley's does not develop what I suppose
should be called the narrative context of his emotion, which
therefore remains incommunicable.

Moreover, these two sorts of accounting, so long as they remain discrete, both work to keep the problem abstract, all in the mind. They are both, in different ways, internal to the mind. The real occasions of the problems are not admitted into consideration. In Shelley's poem, this may be caused by a despairing acceptance of loneliness. In the Nuclear Regulatory Commission deliberations it is caused, I think, by fear; the commissioners take refuge in the impersonality of technological procedures. They cannot bear to acknowledge considerations and feelings that might break the insulating spell of their "objective" dispassion.

Or, to put it another way, their language and their way of thought make it possible for them to think of the crisis only as a technical event or problem. Even a meltdown is fairly understandable and predictable within the terms of their expertise. What is unthinkable is the evacuation of a massively populated region. It is the disorder, confusion, and uncertainty of that exodus that they cannot face. In dealing with the unstudied failure mode, the commissioners' minds do not have to leave their meeting room. It is an *internal* problem. The other, the human, possibility, if they were really to deal with it, would send them shouting into the streets. Even worse, perhaps, from the point of view of their discipline, it would force them to face the absurdity of the idea of "emergency planning"—the idea, in other words, of a controlled catastrophe. They would have to admit, against all the claims of professional standing and "job security," that the only way to control the danger of a nuclear power plant is not to build it. That is to say, if they had a language strong and fine enough to consider *all* the considerations, it would tend to force them out of the confines of "objective" thought and into action, out of solitude into community.

It is the *purity* of objective thought that finally seduces and destroys it. The same thing happens, it seems to me, to the subjective mind. For certain emotions, especially the extremely subjective ones of self-pity and self-love, isolation holds a strong enticement: it offers to keep them pure and neat, aloof from the disorderliness and the mundane obligations of the human common ground.

The only way, so far as I can see, to achieve an accounting that is verifiably and reliably external is to admit the internal, the personal, as an appropriate, necessary consideration. If the Nuclear Regulatory Commissioners, for example, had spoken a good common English, instead of the languages of their specialization and of public relations, then they might have spoken of their personal anxiety and bewilderment, and so brought into consideration what they had in common with the people whose health and lives they were responsible for. They might, in short, have sympathized openly with those people—and so have understood the probably unbearable burden of their public trusteeship.

To be bound within the confines of either the internal or the external way of accounting is to be diseased. To hold the two in balance is to validate both kinds, and to have health. I am not using these terms "disease" and "health" according to any clinical definitions, but am speaking simply from my own observation that when my awareness of how I feel overpowers my awareness of where I am and who is there with me, I am sick, diseased. This can be appropriately extended to say that if what I think obscures my sense of whereabouts and company, I am diseased. And the converse is also true: I am diseased if I become so aware of my surroundings that my own inward life is obscured, as if I should so fix upon the value of some mineral in the ground as to forget that the world is God's work and my home.

But still another example is necessary, and other terms.

In an article entitled "The Evolution and Future of American Animal Agriculture," G. W. Salisbury and R. G. Hart[14] consider the transformation of American agriculture "from an art form into a science." The difference, they say, is that the art of agriculture is concerned "only" with the "how . . . of farming," whereas the science is interested in the "whys."

As an example—or, as they say, a "reference index"—of this change, the authors use the modern history of milk production: the effort, from their point of view entirely successful, "to change the dairy cow from the family companion animal she became after domestication and through all of man's subsequent history into an appropriate manufacturing unit of the twentieth century for the efficient transformation of unprocessed feed into food for man."

The authors produce "two observations" about this change, and these constitute their entire justification of it:

> First, the total cow population was reduced in the period 1944 through 1975 by 67 percent, but second, the yield per cow during the same period increased by 60 percent. In practical terms, the research that yielded such dramatic gains produced a savings for the American public as a whole of approximately 50 billion pounds of total digestible nitrogen per year in the production of a relatively constant level of milk.

The authors proceed to work this out in dollar values, and to say that the quantity of saved dollars finally "gets to the point that people simply do not believe it." And later they say that, in making this change, "The major disciplines were genetics, reproduction, and nutrition."

This is obviously a prime example of internal accounting in the economic sense. The external account is not fully renderable; the context of the accounting is vast, some quantities are not known, and some of the costs are not quantifiable. However, there can be no question that the externalized costs are large. The net gain is not, as these authors imply, identical with the gross. And the industrialization of milk production is a part of a much larger enterprise that may finally produce a highly visible, if not entirely computable, net loss.

At least two further observations are necessary:

1. The period, 1944–1975, also saw a drastic decrease in the

number of dairies, by reason of the very change cited by Salisbury and Hart. The smaller—invariably the smaller—dairies were forced out because of the comparative "inefficiency" of their "manufacturing units." Their failure was part of a major population shift, which seriously disrupted the life both of the country communities and of the cities, broke down traditional community forms, and so on.

2. The industrialization of agriculture, of which the industrialization of milk production is a part, has caused serious problems that even agricultural specialists are beginning to recognize: soil erosion, soil compaction, chemical poisoning and pollution, energy shortages, several kinds of money troubles, obliteration of plant and animal species, disruption of soil biology.

The human, the agricultural, and the ecological costs are all obviously great. Some of them have begun to force their way into the accounts and are straining the economy. Others are, and are likely to remain, external to all ledgers.

The passages I have quoted from Professors Salisbury and Hart provide a very neat demonstration of the shift from a balanced internal-external accounting (the dairy cow as "family companion animal") to a so-called "objective" accounting (the dairy cow as "appropriate manufacturing unit of the twentieth century"), which is, in fact, internal to an extremely limited definition of agricultural progress.

The discarded language, oddly phrased though it is, comes close to a kind of accountability: the internal (family) and the external (cow) are joined by a moral connection (companionship). A proof of its accountability is that this statement can be the basis of moral behavior: "Be good to the cow, for she is our companion."

The preferred phrase—"appropriate manufacturing unit of the twentieth century"—has nothing of this accountability. One can say, of course: "Be good to the cow, for she is productive (or expensive)." But that could be said of a machine; it takes no account of the cow as a living, much less a fellow, creature. But the phrase is equally unaccountable as language. "Appropriate" to what? Though the authors write "appropriate . . . of the twentieth century," they may mean "appropriate . . . *to* the twentieth century." But are there no families and no needs for companionship with animals in the twentieth century? Or perhaps they mean "appropriate . . . for the efficient transformation of unprocessed feed into food for man." But the problem remains. Who is this "man"? Someone, perhaps, who needs no companionship with family or animals? We are constrained to suppose so, for "objectivity" has apparently eliminated "family" and "companion " as terms subject to personal bias—perhaps as "merely sentimental." By the terms of this "objective" accounting, then, "man" is a creature who needs to eat, and who is for some unspecified reason more important than a cow. But for a reader who considers himself a "man" by any broader definition, this language is virtually meaningless. Because the terms of personal bias (that is, the terms of *value*) have been eliminated, the terms of judgment ("appropriate" and "efficient") mean nothing. The authors' conditions would be just as well satisfied if the man produced the milk and the cow bought it, or if a machine produced it and a machine bought it.

Sense, and the possibility of sense, break down here because too much that clearly belongs in has been left out. Like the Nuclear Regulatory Commissioners, Salisbury and Hart have eliminated themselves as representative human beings, and they go on to eliminate the cow as a representative animal—all "interests" are thus removed from the computation. They scrupulously pluck out the representative or symbolic terms in order to achieve a pristinely "objective" accounting of the performance of a "unit." And so we are astonished to discover, at the end of this process, that they have complacently allowed the dollar to stand as representative of *all* value. What announced itself as a statement about animal agriculture has become, by way of several obscure changes of subject, a crudely simplified statement about industrial economics. This is not, in any respectable sense, language, or thought, or even computation. Like the textbooks I have discussed, and like the dialogue of the Nuclear Regulatory Commission, it is a pretentious and dangerous deception, forgiveable only insofar as it may involve self-deception.

If we are to begin to make a reliable account of it, this recent history of milk production must be seen as occurring within a system of nested systems: the individual human within the family within the community within agriculture within nature:

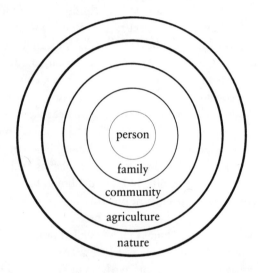

So long as the smaller systems are enclosed within the larger, and so long as all are connected by complex patterns of interdependency, as we know they are, then whatever affects one system will affect the others.

It seems that this system of systems is safe so long as each system is controlled by the next larger one. If at any point the hierarchy is reversed, and the smaller begins to control the larger, then the destruction of the entire system of systems begins. This system of systems is perhaps an updated, ecological version of the Great Chain of Being. That is, it may bring us back to a hierarchical structure not too different from the one that underlies *Paradise Lost*—a theory of the form of Creation which is at the same time a moral form, and which is violated by the "disobedience" or *hubris* of attempting to rise and take power above one's proper place.

But the sketch I have made of the system of systems is much too crude, for the connections between systems, insofar as this is a human structure, are not "given" or unconscious or automatic, but involve disciplines. Persons are joined to families, families to communities, etc., by disciplines that must be deliberately made, remembered, taught, learned, and practiced.

The system of systems begins to disintegrate when the hierarchy is reversed because that begins the disintegration of the connecting disciplines. Disciplines, typically, degenerate into professions, professions into careers. The accounting of Salisbury and Hart is defective because it upsets the hierarchies and so, perhaps unwittingly, fails to consider all the necessary considerations. Their "reference index" does occur within a system of systems—but a drastically abbreviated one, which involves a serious distortion:

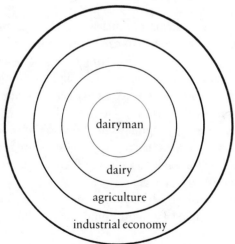

Two things are wrong with this. First, too much has been left out; the claims of family, community, and nature are all ignored. Second, the outer circle is too much within the interest of the inner. The dairyman is not *necessarily* under the control of simple greed—but this structure supplies no hint of a reason why he should not be.

The system of systems, as I first described it, involves three different kinds of interests:

1. The ontogenetic. This is self-interest and is at the center.

2. The phylogenetic. This is the interest that we would call "humanistic." It reaches through family and community and into agriculture. But it does not reach far enough into agriculture because, by its own terms, it cannot.

3. The ecogenetic. This is the interest of the whole "household" in which life is lived. (I don't know whether I invented this term or not. If I did, I apologize.)

These terms give us another way to characterize the flaw in the accounting of Salisbury and Hart. Their abbreviated system of systems fails either to assemble enough facts, to account fully for the meaning of the facts, or to provide any standard of judgment, because the ontogenetic interest is both internal and external to it.

The system of systems, as I first sketched it, has this vulnerability: that the higher interests can be controlled or exploited by the lower interests simply by leaving things out—a procedure just as available to ignorance as to the highest cunning of "applied science." And given even the most generous motives, ignorance is always going to be involved.

There is no reliable standard for behavior anywhere within the system of systems except truth. Lesser standards produce destruction—as, for example, the standards of public relations make gibberish of language.

The trouble, obviously, is that we do not know much of the truth. In particular, we know comparatively little ecogenetic truth.

And so yet another term has to be introduced. The system of

systems has to be controlled from above and outside. There has to be a religious interest of some kind above the ecogenetic. It will be sufficient to my purpose to say simply that the system of systems is enclosed within mystery, in which some truth can be known, but never all truth.

Neither the known truth nor the mystery is internal to any system. And here, however paradoxical it may seem, we begin to see a possibility of reliable accounting and of responsible behavior. The appropriateness of words or deeds can be determined only in reference to the whole "household" in which they occur. But this whole, as such, cannot enter into the accounting. (If it could, then the only necessary language would be mathematics, and the only necessary discipline would be military.) It can only come in as mystery: a factor of X which stands not for the unknown but the unknowable. This is an X that cannot be solved—which may be thought a disadvantage by some; its advantage is that, once it has been let into the account, it cannot easily be ignored. You cannot leave anything out of mystery, because by definition everything is always in it.

The practical use of religion, then, is to keep the accounting in as large a context as possible—to see, in fact, that the account is never "closed." Religion forces the accountant to reckon with mystery—the unsolvable X that keeps the debit and credit or cost and benefit columns open so that no "profit" can ever be safely declared. It forces the accounting outside of every enclosure that it might be internal to. Practically, this X means that all "answers" must be worked out within a limit of humility and restraint, so that the initiative to act would always imply a knowing acceptance of accountability for the results. The establishment and maintenance of this limit seems to me the ultimate empirical problem—the real "frontier" of science, or at least of the definition of the possibility of a *moral* science. It would place science under the rule of the old concern for propriety, correct proportion, proper scale—from which, in modern times, even the arts have been "liberated." That is, it would return to all work, artistic or scientific, the possibility of an external standard of quality. The quality of work or of a made thing would be determined by how conservingly it fitted into the system of systems. Judgment could then begin to articulate what is already obvious: that some work preserves the household of life, and some work destroys it. And thus a real liberation could take place: life and work could go free of those "professional standards" (and professional languages) that are invariably destructive of quality, because they always work as sheep's clothing for various kinds of ontogenetic motives. It is because of these professional standards that the industries and governments, while *talking* of the "betterment of the human condition," can *act* to enrich and empower themselves.

The connections within the system of systems are *practical* connections. The practicality consists in the realization that—despite the blandishments of the various short-circuited "professional" languages—you cannot speak or act in your own best interest without espousing and serving a higher interest. It is not knowledge that enforces this realization, but the humbling awareness of the insufficiency of knowledge, of mystery.

Applying, then, the standard of ecogenetic health to the work of Salisbury and Hart, we get a third way to describe its failure: it makes a principle of replacing the complex concern for quality ("how") with the drastically simplifying concern for quantity. Thus motive is entirely "liberated" from method: any way is good so long as it increases per unit production. But everything except production is diminished in the process, and Salisbury and Hart do not have a way of accounting for, hence no ability even to recognize, these diminishments. All that has been diminished could have been protected by a lively interest in the question of "how," which Salisbury and Hart—like the interests they are accounting for—rule out at the beginning. They were nevertheless working under what I take to be a rule: When you subtract quality from quantity, the gross result is not a net gain.

And so a reliable account is personal at the beginning and religious at the end. This does not mean that a reliable account includes the whole system of systems, for no account can do that. It does mean that the account is made in precise reference to the system of systems—which is another way of saying that it is made in respect for it. Without this respect for the larger structures, the accounting shrinks into the confines of some smaller structure and becomes specialized, partial, and destructive.

It is this sort of external accounting that deals with connections and thus inevitably raises the issue of quality. Which, I take it, is always the same as the issue of propriety: how appropriate is the tool to the work, the work to the need, the need to other needs and the needs of others, and to the health of the household or community of all creatures?

And this kind of accounting gives us the great structures of poetry—as in Homer, Dante, and Milton. It is these great structures, I think, that carry us into the sense of being, in Gary Snyder's phrase, "at one with each other."[15] They teach us to imagine the life that is divided from us by difference or enmity: as Homer imagined the "enemy" hero, Hector; as Dante, on his pilgrimage to Heaven, imagined the damned; as Milton, in his awed study of the meaning of obedience, epitomized sympathetically in his Satan the disobedient personality. And as, now, ecological insight proposes again a poetry with the power to imagine the lives of animals and plants and streams and stones. And this imagining is eminently proprietous, fitting to the claims and privileges of the great household.

Unlike the problems of quantity, the problems of propriety are never "solved," but are ceaselessly challenging and interesting. This is the antidote to the romance of big technological solutions. Life would be interesting—there would be exciting work to do—even if there were no nuclear power plants or "agri-industries" or space adventures. The elaborations of elegance are at least as fascinating, and more various, more democratic, more healthy, more practical—though less glamorous—than elaborations of power.

Without this ultimate reference to the system of systems, and this ultimate concern for quality, any rendering of account falls into the service of a kind of tyranny: it accompanies, and in one way or another invariably enables, the taking of power, from people first and last, but also from all other created things.

In this degenerative accounting, language is almost without the power of designation because it is used conscientiously to refer to nothing in particular. Attention rests upon percentages, categories, abstract functions. The reference drifts inevitably toward the merely provisional. It is not language that the user will very likely be required to stand by or to act on, for it does not define any personal ground for standing or acting. Its only practical utility is to support with "expert opinion" a vast, impersonal technological action already begun. And it works directly against the conventionality, the community life, of language, for it holds in contempt, not only all particular grounds of private fidelity and action, but the common ground of human experience, memory, and understanding from which language rises and on which meaning is shaped. It is a tyrannical language: tyrannese.

Do people come consciously to such language and to such implicit purpose? I hope not. I do not think so. It seems likely to me that, first, a certain kind of confusion must occur. It is a confusion about the human place in the universe, and it has been produced by diligent "educational" labors. This confusion is almost invariably founded on some romantic proposition about the "high destiny of man" or "unlimited human horizons." For an example I turn to R. Buckminster Fuller,[16] here defending the "cosmic realism" of space colonization:

> Conceptualizing realistically about humans as passengers on board 8,000-mile diameter Spaceship Earth traveling around the Sun at 60,000 miles an hour while flying formation with the Moon, which

formation involves the 365 revolutions per each Sun circuit, and recalling that humans have always been born naked, helpless and ignorant though superbly equipped cerebrally, and endowed with
hunger, thirst, curiosity and procreative instincts, it has been logical
for humans to employ their minds' progressive discoveries of the
cosmic principles governing all physical interattractions, interactions, reactions and intertransformings, and to use those principles
in progressively organizing, to humanity's increasing advantage, the
complex of cosmic principles interacting locally to produce their in-
itial environment which most probably was that of a verdant south
seas coral atoll—built by the coral on a volcano risen from ocean bottom ergo unoccupied by any animals, having only fish and birds as
well as fruits, nuts and coconut milk.

That is a single sentence. I call attention not only to the vague-
ness and oversimplification of its generalities, but, more important, to the weakness of its grammar and the shapelessness and
aimlessness of its syntax. The subject is an "it" of very tentative
reference, buried in the middle of the sentence—an "it," moreover, that cannot possibly be the subject of the two complicated
participial constructions that precede it. The sentence, then, begins with a dangling modifier half its length. On the other end, it
peters out in a description of the biology of a coral atoll, the per-
tinence of which is never articulated. In general, the sentence is a
labyrinth of syntactical confusions impossible to map. When we
reflect that "sentence" means, literally, "a way of thinking"
(Latin: *sententia*) and that it comes from the Latin *sentire*, to
feel, we realize that the concepts of sentence and sentence structure are not merely grammatical or merely academic—not neg-
ligible in any sense. A sentence is both the opportunity and the
limit of thought—what we have to think with, and what we have
to think in. It is, moreover, a *feelable* thought, a thought that im-
presses its sense not just on our understanding, but on our hear-
ing, our sense of rhythm and proportion. It is a pattern of felt
sense.

A sentence that is completely shapeless is therefore a loss of thought, an act of self-abandonment to incoherence. And indeed Mr. Fuller shows himself here a man who conceives a sentence, not as a pattern of thought apprehensible to sense, but merely as a clot of abstract concepts. In such a syntactical clot, words and concepts will necessarily tend to function abstractly rather than referentially. It is the statement of a man for whom words have replaced things, and who has therefore ceased to think particularly about any thing.

The idea buried in all those words is, so far as I can tell, a simple one: humans are born earth-bound, ignorant, and vulnerable, but intelligent; by their intelligence they lift themselves up from their primitive origin and move to fulfill their destiny. As we learn in later sentences, this destiny is universal in scope, limitless ("ever larger"), and humans are to approach it by larger and larger technology. The end is not stated, obviously, because it is not envisioned, because it is not envisionable. It seems to me that the aimlessness, the limitlessness, of Mr. Fuller's idea produces the aimlessness and shapelessness of his sentence.

By contrast, consider another view of the human place in the universe, not a simple view or simply stated, but nevertheless comely, orderly, and clear:

> There wanted yet the Master work, the end
> Of all yet done: A Creature who not prone
> And Brute as other Creatures, but endu'd
> With Sanctity of Reason, might erect
> His Stature, and upright with Front serene
> Govern the rest, self-knowing, and from thence
> Magnanimous to correspond with Heav'n,
> But grateful to acknowledge whence his good
> Descends, thither with heart and voice and eyes
> Directed in Devotion to adore
> And worship God Supreme . . .[17]

These lines of Milton immediately suggest what is wrong, first, with Mr. Fuller's sentence, and then with the examples of tyrannese that preceded it. They all assume that the human prerogative is unlimited, that we *must* do whatever we have the power to do. Specifically, what is lacking is the idea that humans have a place in Creation and that this place is limited by responsibility on the one hand and by humility on the other—or, in Milton's terms, by magnanimity and devotion. Without this precision of definition, this setting of bounds or ends to thought, we cannot mean, or say what we mean, or mean what we say; we cannot stand by our words because we cannot utter words that can be stood by; we cannot speak of our own actions as persons, or even as communities, but only of the actions of percentages, large organizations, concepts, historical trends, or the impersonal "forces" of destiny or evolution.

Or let us consider another pair of statements. The first, again from Buckminster Fuller, following the one just quoted, elaborates his theme of technological destiny:

> First the humans developed fish catching and carving tools, then rafts, dug-out canoes and paddles and then sailing outrigger canoes.
> Reaching the greater islands and the mainland they developed animal skin, grass and leafwoven clothing and skin tents. They gradually entered safely into geographical areas where they would previously have perished. Slowly they learned to tame, then breed, cows, bullocks, water buffalo, horses and elephants. Next they developed oxen, then horse-drawn vehicles, then horseless vehicles, then ships of the sky. Then employing rocketry and packaging up the essential life-supporting environmental constituents of the biosphere they made sorties away from their mothership Earth and finally ferried over to their Sun orbiting-companion, the Moon.

The other is from William Faulkner's story, "The Bear."[18] Isaac McCaslin is speaking of his relinquishment of the ownership of land:

> He created the earth, made it and looked at it and said it was all right, and then He made man. He made the earth first and peopled it with dumb creatures, and then He created man to be His overseer on the earth and to hold suzerainty over the earth and the animals on it in His name, not to hold for himself and his descendants inviolable title forever, generation after generation, to the oblongs and squares of

the earth, but to hold the earth mutual and intact in the communal anonymity of brotherhood, and all the fee He asked was pity and humility and sufferance and endurance and the sweat of his face for bread.

The only continuity recognized by Mr. Fuller is that of technological development, which is in fact not a continuity at all, for, as he sees it, it does not proceed by building on the past but by outmoding and replacing it. And if any other human concern accompanied the development from canoe to spaceship, it is either not manifest to Mr. Fuller, or he does not think it important enough to mention.

The passage from Faulkner, on the other hand, cannot be understood except in terms of the historical and cultural continuity that produced it. It awakens our memory of Genesis and *Paradise Lost*, as *Paradise Lost* awakens our memory of Genesis. In each of these the human place in Creation is described as a moral circumstance, and this circumstance is understood each time, it seems to me, with a deeper sense of crisis, as history has proved humanity more and more the exploiter and destroyer of Creation rather than its devout suzerain or steward. Milton knew of the conquests of Africa and the Americas, the brutality of which had outraged the humane minds of Europe and provided occasion to raise again the question of the human place in Creation; the devils of *Paradise Lost* are, among other things, conquistadores. (They are also the most expedient of politicians and technologists: ". . . by strength / They measure all. . . .") Faulkner's Isaac McCaslin, a white Mississippian of our own time, speaks not just with Milton's passion as a moral witness, but with the anguish of a man who inherits directly the guilt of the conqueror, the history of expropriation, despoliation, and slavery.

It is of the greatest importance to see how steadfastly this thrust of tradition, from Genesis to Milton to Faulkner, works toward the definition of personal place and condition, responsibility and action. And one feels the potency of this tradition to reach past the negativity of Isaac McCaslin's too simple relinquishment toward the definition of the atoning and renewing work that each person must do. Mr. Fuller's vision, by contrast, proposes that we have ahead of us only the next technological "breakthrough"—which, now that we have "progressed" to the scale of spaceships, is not work for persons or communities but for governments and corporations. We have in these two statements an open conflict between unlimited technology and traditional value. It is foolish to think that these are compatible. Value and technology can meet only on the ground of restraint.

The technological determinists have tyrannical attitudes, and speak tyrannese, at least partly because their assumptions cannot produce a moral or a responsible definition of the human place in Creation. Because they assume that the human place is any place, they are necessarily confused about where they belong.

Where does this confusion come from? I think it comes from the specialization and abstraction of intellect, separating it from responsibility and humility, magnanimity and devotion, and thus giving it an importance that, in the order of things and in its own nature, it does not and cannot have. The specialized intellectual assumes, in other words, that intelligence is all in the mind. For illustration, I turn again to *Paradise Lost*, where Satan, fallen, boasts in "heroic" defiance that he has

> A mind not to be chang'd by Place or Time.
> The mind is its own place, and in itself
> Can make a Heav'n of Hell, a Hell of Heav'n,
> What matter where, if I be still the same . . .[19]

I do not know where one could find a better motto for the modernist or technological experiment, which assumes that we can fulfill a high human destiny anywhere, any way, so long as we can keep up the momentum of innovation; that the mind is "its own place" even within ecological degradation, pollution, poverty, hatred, and violence.

What we know, on the contrary, is that in any culture that could be called healthy or sane we find a much richer, larger concept of intelligence. We find, first, some way of acknowledging in action the existence of "higher intelligence." And we find that the human mind, in such a culture, is invariably strongly *placed*, in reference to other minds in the community and in cultural memory and tradition, and in reference to earthly localities and landmarks. Intelligence survives both by internal coherence and external pattern; it is both inside and outside the mind. People are born both with and into intelligence. What is thought refers precisely to what is thought about. It is this outside intelligence that we are now ignoring and consequently destroying.

As industrial technology advances and enlarges, and in the process assumes greater social, economic, and political force, it carries people away from where they belong by history, culture, deeds, association, and affection. And it destroys the landmarks by which they might return. Often it destroys the nature or the character of the places they have left. The very possibility of a practical connection between thought and the world is thus destroyed. Culture is driven into the mind, where it cannot be preserved. Displaced memory, for instance, is hard to keep in mind, harder to hand down. The little that survives is attenuated — without practical force. That is why the Jews, in Babylon, wept when they remembered Zion. The mere memory of a place cannot preserve it, nor apart from the place itself can it long survive in the mind. "How shall we sing the Lord's song in a strange land?"

The enlargement of industrial technology is thus analogous to war. It continually requires the movement of knowledge and responsibility away from home. It thrives upon the disintegration of homes, the subjugation of homelands. It requires that people cease to cooperate directly to fulfill local needs from local sources and begin instead to deal with each other always across the rift that divides producer and consumer, and always competitively. The idea of the independence of individual farms, shops, communities, and households is anathema to industrial technologists. The rush to nuclear energy and the growth of the space colony idea are powered by the industrial will to cut off the possibility of a small-scale energy technology—which is to say the possibility of small-scale personal and community acts. The corporate producers and their sycophants in the universities and the government will do virtually anything (or so they have obliged us to assume) to keep people from acquiring necessities in any way except by *buying* them.

Industrial technology and its aspirations enlarge along a line described by changes of verb tense: I need this tool; I will need this tool; I would need this tool. The conditional verb rests by nature upon *ifs*. The ifs of technological rationalization (*if* there were sufficient demand, money, knowledge, energy, power) act as wedges between history and futurity, inside and outside, value and desire, and ultimately between people and the earth and between one person and another.

By such shifts in the tenses of thought (as sometimes also by the substitution of the indefinite for the definite article) it is possible to impair or destroy the power of language to designate, to shift the focus of reference from what is outside the mind to what is inside it. And thus what already exists is devalued, subjugated, or destroyed for the sake of what *might* exist. The modern cult of planners and "futurologists" has thus achieved a startling resemblance to Swift's "academy of projectors":[20]

> In these colleges, the professors contrive new rules and methods of agriculture and building, and new instruments and tools for all trades and manufactures; whereby, as they undertake, one man shall do the work of ten: a palace may be built in a week, of materials so durable, as to last for ever without repairing. All the fruits of the earth shall come to maturity, at whatever season we think fit to chuse, and encrease an hundred fold more than they do at present, with innumerable other happy proposals. The only inconvenience is, that none of these projects are yet brought to perfection; and, in the mean time, the whole country lies miserably waste. . . .

People who are willing to follow technology wherever it leads are necessarily willing to follow it away from home, off the earth, and outside the sphere of human definition, meaning, and responsibility. One has to suppose that this would be all right if they did it only for themselves and if they accepted the terms of their technological romanticism absolutely—that is, if they would depart absolutely from all that they propose to supersede, never to return. But past a certain scale, as C. S. Lewis wrote,[21] the person who makes a technological choice does not choose for himself alone, but for others; past a certain scale, he chooses for *all* others. Past a certain scale, if the break with the past is great enough, he chooses for the past, and if the effects are lasting enough he chooses for the future. He makes, then, a choice that can neither be chosen against nor unchosen. Past a certain scale, there is no dissent from a technological choice.

People speaking out of this technological willingness cannot speak precisely, for what they are talking about does not yet exist. They cannot mean what they say because their words are avowedly speculative. They cannot stand by their words because they are talking about, if not *in*, the future, where they are not standing and cannot stand until long after they have spoken. All the grand and perfect dreams of the technologists are happening in the future, but nobody is there.

What can turn us from this deserted future, back into the sphere of our being, the great dance that joins us to our home, to each other and to other creatures, to the dead and the unborn? I think it is love. I am perforce aware how badly and embarrassingly that word now lies on the page—for we have learned at once to overuse it, abuse it, and hold it in suspicion. But I do not mean any kind of abstract love, which is probably a contradiction in terms, but particular love for particular things, places, creatures, and people, requiring stands and acts, showing its successes or failures in practical or tangible effects. And it implies a responsibility just as particular, not grim or merely dutiful, but rising out of generosity. I think that this sort of love defines the effective range of human intelligence, the range within

which its works can be dependably beneficent. Only the action
that is moved by love for the good at hand has the hope of being
responsible and generous. Desire for the future produces words
that cannot be stood by. But love makes language exact, because
one loves only what one knows. One cannot love the future or
anything in it, for nothing is known there. And one cannot un-
selfishly make a future for someone else. Love for the future is
self-love—love for the present self, projected and magnified into
the future, and it is an irremediable loneliness.

Because love is not abstract, it does not lead to trends or percentages or general behavior. It leads, on the contrary, to the perception that there is no such thing as general behavior. There is
no abstract action. Love proposes the work of settled households and communities, whose innovations come about in response to immediate needs and immediate conditions, as opposed to the work of governments and corporations, whose
innovations are produced out of the implicitly limitless desire
for future power or profit. This difference is the unacknowl-
edged cultural break in Mr. Fuller's evolutionary series: oxen,
horse-drawn vehicles, horseless vehicles, ships of the sky. Between horse-drawn vehicles and horseless vehicles, human life
disconnected itself from local sources; energy started to flow
away from home. A biological limit was overrun, and with it the
deepest human propriety.

Or, to shift the terms, love defines the difference between the
"global village" which is a technological and a totalitarian ideal,
directly suited to the purposes of centralized governments and
corporations, and the Taoist village-as-globe, where the people
live frugally and at peace, pleased with the good qualities of necessary things, so satisfied where they are that they live and die
without visiting the next village, though they can hear its dogs
bark and its roosters crow.[22]

We might conjecture and argue a long time about the meaning
and even the habitability of such a village. But one thing, I think,

is certain: it would not be a linguistic no-man's-land in which words and things, words and deeds, words and people failed to stand in reliable connection or fidelity to one another. People and other creatures would be known by their names and histories, not by their numbers or percentages. History would be handed down in songs and stories, not reduced to evolutionary or technological trends. Generalizations would exist, of course, but they would be distilled from experience, not "projected" from statistics. They would sound, says Lao Tzu,[23] this way:

> "Alert as a winter-farer on an icy stream,"
> "Wary as a man in ambush,"
> "Considerate as a welcome guest,"
> "Selfless as melting ice,"
> "Green as an uncut tree,"
> "Open as a valley . . ."

I come, in conclusion, to the difference between "projecting" the future and making a promise. The "projecting" of "futurologists" *uses* the future as the safest possible context for whatever is desired; it binds one only to selfish interest. But making a promise binds one *to someone else's future*. If the promise is serious enough, one is brought to it by love, and in awe and fear. Fear, awe, and love bind us to no selfish aims, but to each other. And they enforce a speech more exact, more clarifying, and more binding than any speech that can be used to sell or advocate some "future." For when we promise in love and awe and fear there is a certain kind of mobility that we give up. We give up the romanticism of progress, that is always shifting its terms to fit its occasions. We are speaking where we stand, and we shall stand afterwards in the presence of what we have said.

NOTES

1. Harcourt Brace Jovanovich, 1975, pp. 291–303, 235.
2. Harcourt, Brace & World, 1970, pp. 203–211.

3. "Poetry, Community, & Climax," *Field* 20, Spring 1979, p. 29.

4. 1:23 & 24.

5. *Confucius*, New Directions, 1951, pp. 89, 191.

6. E. P. Dutton, 1979, p. 61.

7. *Op. cit.*, p. 21.

8. T. S. Eliot, *The Complete Poems and Plays*, Harcourt, Brace and Company, 1952, p. 235.

9. T. S. Eliot, *Selected Essays*, Harcourt, Brace and Company, 1950, p. 269.

10. W. W. Norton & Company, Volume 2, 1962, pp. 418–419.

11. *Second Defense of the People of England, The Works of John Milton*, Vol. VIII, Columbia University Press, 1933, pp. 249–251.

12. I am indebted, for a useful sampling from these transcripts and a perceptive commentary on them, to Paul Trachtman, "Phenomena, comment, and notes," *Smithsonian*, July 1979, pp. 14–16.

13. Genesis 11:1–9.

14. *Perspectives in Biology and Medicine*, Spring 1979, pp. 394–409.

15. *Op. cit.*, p. 34.

16. *Space Colonies*, edited by Stewart Brand, Penguin, 1977, p. 55.

17. *Paradise Lost*, VII, 505–515.

18. *Go Down Moses*, The Modern Library, 1955, p. 257.

19. I, 253–256.

20. *Gulliver's Travels*, Everyman's Library, 1961, p. 189.

21. *The Abolition of Man*, Macmillan, 1975, pp. 70–71.

22. *Tao Te Ching*, 80.

23. *Ibid.*, 15. (Witter Bynner translation.)

3 People, Land, and Community

I would like to speak more precisely than I have before of the connections that join people, land, and community—to describe, for example, the best human use of a problematical hillside farm. In a healthy culture, these connections are complex. The industrial economy breaks them down by oversimplifying them and in the process raises obstacles that make it hard for us to see what the connections are or ought to be. These are mental obstacles, of course, and there appear to be two major ones: the assumption that knowledge (information) can be "sufficient," and the assumption that time and work are short.

These assumptions will be found implicit in a whole set of contemporary beliefs: that the future can be studied and planned for; that limited supplies can be wasted without harm; that good intentions can safeguard the use of nuclear power. A recent newspaper article says, for example, "A congressionally mandated study of the Ogallala Aquifer is finding no great cause for alarm from [sic] its rapidly dropping levels. The director of the . . . study . . . says that even at current rates of pumping, the aquifer can supply the Plains with water for another forty to fifty years. . . . All six states participating in the study . . . are forecasting increased farm yields based on improved technology." Another article speaks of a different technology with the same optimism: "The nation has invested hundreds of billions of dollars in atomic weapons and at the same time has developed the most sophisticated strategies to fine-tune their use to avoid a holocaust. Yet the system that is meant to activate them is the weakest link in the chain. . . . Thus, some have suggested that what may be needed are warning systems for the warning systems."

Always the assumption is that we can first set demons at large, and then, somehow, become smart enough to control them. This is not childishness. It is not even "human weakness." It is a kind of idiocy, but perhaps we will not cope with it and save ourselves until we regain the sense to call it evil.

The trouble, as in our conscious moments we all know, is that we are terrifyingly ignorant. The most learned of us are ignorant. The acquisition of knowledge always involves the revelation of ignorance—almost *is* the revelation of ignorance. Our knowledge of the world instructs us first of all that the world is greater than our knowledge of it. To those who rejoice in the abundance and intricacy of Creation, this is a source of joy, as it is to those who rejoice in freedom. ("The future comes only by surprise," we say, "—thank God!") To those would-be solvers of "the human problem," who hope for knowledge equal to (capable of controlling) the world, it is a source of unremitting defeat and bewilderment. The evidence is overwhelming that knowledge does not solve "the human problem." Indeed, the evidence overwhelmingly suggests—with Genesis—that knowledge *is* the problem. Or perhaps we should say instead that all our problems tend to gather under two questions about knowledge: Having the ability and desire to know, how and what should we learn? And, having learned, how and for what should we use what we know?

One thing we do know, that we dare not forget, is that better solutions than ours have at times been made by people with much less information than we have. We know too, from the study of agriculture, that the same information, tools, and techniques that in one farmer's hands will ruin land, in another's will save and improve it.

This is not a recommendation of ignorance. To know nothing, after all, is no more possible than to know enough. I am only proposing that knowledge, like everything else, has its place, and that we need urgently now to *put* it in its place. If we want to know and cannot help knowing, then let us learn as fully and accurately as we decently can. But let us at the same time abandon our superstitious beliefs about knowledge: that it is ever sufficient; that it can of itself solve problems; that it is intrinsically good; that it can be used objectively or disinterestedly. Let us acknowledge that the objective or disinterested researcher is always on the side that pays best. And let us give up our forlorn pursuit of the "informed decision."

The "informed decision," I suggest, is as fantastical a creature as the "disinterested third party" and the "objective observer." Or it is if by "informed" we mean "supported by sufficient information." A great deal of our public life, and certainly the most expensive part of it, rests on the assumed possibility of decisions so informed. Examination of private life, however, affords no comfort whatsoever to that assumption. It is simply true that we do not and cannot *know* enough to make any important decision.

Of this dilemma we can take marriage as an instance, for as a condition marriage reveals the insufficiency of knowledge, and as an institution it suggests the possibility that decisions can be informed in another way that *is* sufficient, or approximately so. I take it as an axiom that one cannot know enough to get married, any more than one can predict a surprise. The only people who possess information sufficient to their vows are widows and widowers—who do not know enough to *re*marry.

What is not so well understood now as perhaps it used to be is that marriage is made in an inescapable condition of loneliness and ignorance, to which it, or something like it, is the only possible answer. Perhaps this is so hard to understand now because now the most noted solutions are mechanical solutions, which are often exactly suited to mechanical problems. But we are humans—which means that we not only *have* problems but *are* problems. Marriage is not as nicely trimmed to its purpose as a bottle-stopper; it is a not entirely possible solution to a not entirely soluble problem. And this is true of the other human connections. We can commit ourselves fully to anything—a place, a discipline, a life's work, a child, a family, a community, a faith, a friend—only in the same poverty of knowledge, the same ignorance of result, the same self-subordination, the same final forsaking of other possibilities. If we must make these so final commitments without sufficient information, then what *can* inform our decisions?

In spite of the obvious dangers of the word, we must say first that love can inform them. This, of course, though probably necessary, is not safe. What parent, faced with a child who is in love and going to get married, has not been filled with mistrust and fear—and justly so. We who were lovers before we were parents know what a fraudulent justifier love can be. We know that people stay married for different reasons than those for which they get married and that the later reasons will have to be discovered. Which, of course, is not to say that the later reasons may not confirm the earlier ones; it is to say only that the earlier ones must wait for confirmation.

But our decisions can also be informed—our loves both limited and strengthened—by those patterns of value and restraint, principle and expectation, memory, familiarity, and understanding that, inwardly, add up to *character* and, outwardly, to *culture*. Because of these patterns, and only because of them, we are not alone in the bewilderments of the human condition and human love, but have the company and the comfort of the best of our kind, living and dead. These patterns constitute a knowledge far different from the kind I have been talking about. It is a kind of knowledge that includes information, but is never the same as information. Indeed, if we study the paramount documents of our culture, we will see that this second kind of knowledge invariably implies, and often explicitly imposes, limits upon the first kind: some possibilities must not be explored; some things must not be learned. If we want to get safely home, there are certain seductive songs we must not turn aside for, some sacred things we must not meddle with:

> Great captain,
> a fair wind and the honey lights of home
> are all you seek. But anguish lies ahead;
> the god who thunders on the land prepares it . . .
> . . . .
> One narrow strait may take you through his blows:
> denial of yourself, restraint of shipmates.

This theme, of course, is dominant in Biblical tradition, but the theme itself and its modern inversion can be handily understood by a comparison of this speech of Tirêsias to Odysseus in Robert Fitzgerald's Homer with Tennyson's romantic Ulysses who proposes, like a genetic engineer or an atomic scientist,

> To follow knowledge like a sinking star,
> Beyond the utmost bound of human thought.

Obviously unlike Homer's Odysseus, Tennyson's Ulysses is said to come from Dante, and he does resemble Dante's Ulysses pretty exactly—the critical difference being that Dante thought this Ulysses a madman and a fool, and brings down upon his Tennysonian speech to his sailors one of the swiftest anticlimaxes in literature. The real—the human—knowledge is understood as implying and imposing limits, much as marriage does, and these limits are understood to belong necessarily to the definition of a human being.

In all this talk about marriage I have not forgot that I am supposed to be talking about agriculture. I am going to talk directly about agriculture in a minute, but I want to insist that I have been talking about it indirectly all along, for the analogy between marriage making and farm making, marriage keeping and farm keeping, is nearly exact. I have talked about marriage as a way of talking about farming because marriage, as a human artifact, has been more carefully understood than farming. The analogy between them is so close, for one thing, because they join us to time in nearly the same way. In talking about time, I will begin to talk directly about farming, but as I do so, the reader will be aware, I hope, that I am talking indirectly about marriage.

When people speak with confidence of the longevity of diminishing agricultural sources—as when they speak of their good intentions about nuclear power—they are probably not just being gullible or thoughtless; they are likely to be speaking from belief in several tenets of industrial optimism: that life is long, but time and work are short; that every problem will be solved by a "technological breakthrough" before it enlarges to catastrophe; that *any* problem can be solved in a hurry by large applications of urgent emotion, information, and money. It is regrettable that these assumptions should risk correction by disaster when they could be cheaply and safely overturned by the study of any agriculture that has proved durable.

To the farmer, Emerson said, "The landscape is an armory of powers. . . ." As he meant it, the statement may be true, but the metaphor is ill-chosen, for the powers of a landscape are available to human use in nothing like so simple a way as are the powers of an armory. Or let us say, anyhow, that the preparations needed for the taking up of agricultural powers are more extensive and complex than those usually thought necessary for the taking up of arms. And let us add that the motives are, or ought to be, significantly different.

Arms are taken up in fear and hate, but it has not been uncharacteristic for a farmer's connection to a farm to begin in love. This has not always been so ignorant a love as it sometimes is now; but always, no matter what one's agricultural experience may have been, one's connection to a newly bought farm will begin in love that is more or less ignorant. One loves the place because present appearances recommend it, and because they suggest possibilities irresistibly imaginable. One's head, like a lover's, grows full of visions. One walks over the premises, saying, "If this were mine, I'd make a permanent pasture here; here is where I'd plant an orchard; here is where I'd dig a pond." These visions are the usual stuff of unfulfilled love and induce wakefulness at night.

When one buys the farm and moves there to live, something different begins. Thoughts begin to be translated into acts. Truth begins to intrude with its matter-of-fact. One's work may be defined in part by one's visions, but it is defined in part too by problems, which the work leads to and reveals. And daily life, work, and problems gradually alter the visions. It invariably turns out, I think, that one's first vision of one's place was to some extent an imposition on it. But if one's sight is clear and if one stays on and works well, one's love gradually responds to the place as it really is, and one's visions gradually image possibilities that are really in it. Vision, possibility, work, and life—*all* have changed by mutual correction. Correct discipline, given enough time, gradually removes one's self from one's line of sight. One works to better purpose then and makes fewer mistakes, because at last one sees where one is. Two human possibilities of the highest order thus come within reach: what one wants can become the same as what one has, and one's knowledge can cause respect for what one knows.

"Correct discipline" and "enough time" are inseparable notions. Correct discipline cannot be hurried, for it is both the knowledge of what ought to be done, and the willingness to do it—*all* of it, properly. The good worker will not suppose that good work can be made properly answerable to haste, urgency, or even emergency. But the good worker knows too that after it is done work requires yet more time to prove its worth. One must stay to experience and study and understand the consequences—must understand them by living with them, and then correct them, if necessary, by longer living and more work. It won't do to correct mistakes made in one place by moving to another place, as has been the common fashion in America, or by adding on another place, as is the fashion in any sort of "growth economy." Seen this way, questions about farming become inseparable from questions about propriety of scale. A farm can be too big for a farmer to husband properly or pay proper attention to. Distraction is inimical to correct discipline, and enough time is beyond the reach of anyone who has too much to do. But we must go farther and see that propriety of scale is invariably associated with propriety of another kind: an understanding and acceptance of the human place in the order of Creation—a proper humility. There are some things the arrogant mind does not see; it is blinded by its vision of what it desires. It does not see what is already there; it never sees the forest that precedes the farm or the farm that precedes the shopping center; it will never understand that America was "discovered" by the Indians. It is the properly humbled mind in its proper place that sees truly, because—to give only one reason—it sees details.

And the good farmer understands that further limits are imposed upon haste by nature which, except for an occasional storm or earthquake, is in no hurry either. In the processes of most concern to agriculture—the building and preserving of fertility—nature is never in a hurry. During the last seventeen years, for example, I have been working at the restoration of a once exhausted hillside. Its scars are now healed over, though still visible, and this year it has provided abundant pasture, more than in any year since we have owned it. But to make it as good as it is now has taken seventeen years. If I had been a millionaire or if my family had been starving, it would still have taken seventeen years. It can be better than it now is, but that will take longer. For it to live fully in its own possibility, as it did before bad use ran it down, may take hundreds of years.

But to think of the human use of a piece of land as continuing through hundreds of years, we must greatly complicate our understanding of agriculture. Let us start a job of farming on a given place—say an initially fertile hillside in the Kentucky River Valley—and construe it through time:

1. To begin using this hillside for agricultural production—pasture or crop—is a matter of a year's work. This is work in the present tense, adequately comprehended by conscious intention and by the first sort of knowledge I talked about—information available to the farmer's memory and built into his methods, tools, and crop and livestock species. Understood in its present tense, the work does not reveal its value except insofar as the superficial marks of craftsmanship may be seen and judged. But excellent workmanship, as with a breaking plow, may prove as damaging as bad workmanship. The work has not revealed its connections to the place or to the worker. These connections are revealed in time.

2. To live on the hillside and use it for a lifetime gives the annual job of work a past and a future. To live on the hillside and use it without diminishing its fertility or wasting it by erosion still requires conscious intention and information, but now we must say *good* intention and *good* (that is, correct) information, resulting in *good* work. And to these we must now add *character*: the sort of knowledge that might properly be called familiarity, and the affections, habits, values, and virtues (conscious and unconscious) that would preserve good care and good work through hard times.

3. For human life to continue on the hillside through successive generations requires good use, good work, all along. For in any agricultural place that will waste or erode—and all will—bad work does not permit "muddling through"; sooner or later it ends human life. Human continuity is virtually synonymous with good farming, and good farming obviously must outlast the life of any good farmer. For it to do this, in addition to the preceding requirements, we must have *community*. Without community, the good work of a single farmer or a single family will not mean much or last long. For good farming to last, it must occur in a good farming community—that is, a neighborhood of people who know each other, who understand their mutual dependences, and who place a proper value on good farming. In its

cultural aspect, the community is an order of memories preserved consciously in instructions, songs, and stories, and both
consciously and unconsciously in *ways*. A healthy culture holds
preserving knowledge *in place* for a *long* time. That is, the essential wisdom accumulates in the community much as fertility
builds in the soil. In both, death becomes potentiality.

People are joined to the land by work. Land, work, people, and
community are all comprehended in the idea of culture. These
connections cannot be understood or described by information—so many resources to be transformed by so many workers
into so many products for so many consumers—because they
are not quantitative. We can understand them only after we acknowledge that they should be harmonious—that a culture
must be either shapely and saving or shapeless and destructive.
To presume to describe land, work, people, and community by
information, by quantities, seems invariably to throw them into
competition with one another. Work is then understood to exploit the land, the people to exploit their work, the community
to exploit its people. And then instead of land, work, people, and
community, we have the industrial categories of resources, labor, management, consumers, and government. We have ex-
changed harmony for an interminable fuss, and the work of culture for the timed and harried labor of an industrial economy.

But let me bring these notions to the trial of a more particular
example.

Wes Jackson and Marty Bender of the Land Institute have recently worked out a comparison between the energy economy of
a farm using draft horses for most of its field work and that of an
identical farm using tractors. This is a project a generation over-
due, of the greatest interest and importance—in short, necessary. And the results will be shocking to those who assume a direct proportion between fossil fuel combustion and human
happiness.

These results, however, have not fully explained one fact that Jackson and Bender had before them at the start of their analysis and that was still running ahead of them at the end: that in the last twenty-five or thirty years, the Old Order Amish, who use horses for farmwork, doubled their population and stayed in farming, whereas in the same period millions of mechanized farmers were driven out. The reason that this is not adequately explained by analysis of the two energy economies, I believe, is that the problem is by its nature beyond the reach of analysis of any kind. The real or whole reason must be impossibly complicated, having to do with nature, culture, religion, family and community life, as well as with agricultural methodology and economics. What I think we are up against is an unresolvable difference between thought and action, thought and life.

What works *poorly* in agriculture—monoculture, for instance, or annual accounting—can be pretty fully explained, because what works poorly is invariably some oversimplifying *thought* that subjugates nature, people, and culture. What works well ultimately defies explanation because it involves an order which in both magnitude and complexity is ultimately incomprehensible.

Here, then, is a prime example of the futility of a dependence on information. We cannot contain what contains us or comprehend what comprehends us. Yeats said that "Man can embody truth but he cannot know it." The part, that is, cannot comprehend the whole, though it can stand for it (and by it). Synecdoche is possible, and its possibility implies the possibility of harmony between part and whole. If we cannot work on the basis of sufficient information, then we have to work on the basis of an understanding of harmony. That, I take it, is what Sir Albert Howard and Wes Jackson mean when they tell us that we must study and emulate on our farms the natural integrities that precede and support agriculture.

The study of Amish agriculture, like the study of *any* durable agriculture, suggests that we live in sequences of patterns that are formally analogous. These sequences are probably hierarchical, at least in the sense that some patterns are more comprehensive than others; they tend to arrange themselves like internesting bowls—though any attempt to represent their order visually will oversimplify it.

And so we must suspect that Amish horse-powered farms work well, not because—or not *just* because—horses are energy-efficient, but because they are living creatures, and therefore fit harmoniously into a pattern of relationships that are necessarily biological, and that rhyme analogically from ecosystem to crop, from field to farmer. In other words, ecosystem, farm, field, crop, horse, farmer, family, and community are in certain critical ways *like* each other. They are, for instance, all related to health and fertility or reproductivity in about the same way. The health and fertility of each involves and is involved in the health and fertility of all.

It goes without saying that tools can be introduced into this agricultural and ecological order without jeopardizing it—but only up to a certain kind, scale, and power. To introduce a tractor into it, as the historical record now seems virtually to prove, is to begin its destruction. The tractor has been so destructive, I think, because it is *unlike* anything else in the agricultural order, and so it breaks the essential harmony. And with the tractor comes dependence on an energy supply that lies not only off the farm but outside agriculture and outside biological cycles and integrities. With the tractor, both farm and farmer become "resources" of the industrial economy, which always exploits its resources.

We would be wrong, of course, to say that anyone who farms with a tractor is a bad farmer. That is not true. What we must say, however, is that once a tractor is introduced into the pattern of a farm, certain necessary restraints and practices, once implicit in technology, must now reside in the character and consciousness of the farmer—at the same time that the economic pressure to cast off restraint and good practice has been greatly increased.

In a society addicted to facts and figures, anyone trying to speak for agricultural *harmony* is inviting trouble. The first trouble is in trying to say what harmony is. It cannot be reduced to facts and figures—though the lack of it can. It is not very visibly a function. Perhaps we can only say what it may be like. It may, for instance, be like sympathetic vibration: "The A string of a violin . . . is designed to vibrate most readily at about 440 vibrations per second: the note A. If that same note is played loudly not on the violin but near it, the violin A string may hum in sympathy." This may have a practical exemplification in the craft of the mud daubers which, as they trowel mud into their nest walls, hum to it, or at it, communicating a vibration that makes it easier to work, thus mastering their material by a kind of song. Perhaps the hum of the mud dauber only activates that anciently perceived likeness between all creatures and the earth of which they are made. For as common wisdom holds, like *speaks to* like. And harmony always involves such specificities of form as in the mud dauber's song and its nest, whereas information accumulates indiscriminately, like noise.

Of course, in the order of creatures, humanity is a special case. Humans, unlike mud daubers, are not naturally involved in harmony. For humans, harmony is always a human product, an artifact, and if they do not know how to make it and choose to make it, then they do not have it. And so I suggest that, for humans, the harmony I am talking about may bear an inescapable likeness to what we know as moral law—or that, for humans, moral law is a significant part of the notation of ecological and agricultural harmony. A great many people seem to have voted for information as a safe substitute for virtue, but this ignores— among much else—the need to prepare humans to live short lives in the face of long work and long time.

Perhaps it is only when we focus our minds on our machines that time seems short. Time is always running out for machines. They shorten our work, in a sense popularly approved, by simplifying it and speeding it up, but our work perishes quickly in them too as they wear out and are discarded. For the living Creation, on the other hand, time is always coming. It is running out for the farm built on the industrial pattern; the industrial farm burns fertility as it burns fuel. For the farm built into the pattern of living things, as an analogue of forest or prairie, time is a bringer of gifts. These gifts may be welcomed and cared for. To some extent they may be expected. Only within strict limits are they the result of human intention and knowledge. They cannot in the usual sense be made. Only in the short term of industrial accounting can they be thought simply earnable. Over the real length of human time, to be earned they must be deserved.

From this rather wandering excursion I arrive at two conclusions.

The first is that the modern stereotype of an intelligent person is probably wrong. The prototypical modern intelligence seems to be that of the Quiz Kid—a human shape barely discernable in fluff of facts. It is understood that everything must be justified by facts, and facts are offered in justification of *everything*. If it is a fact that soil erosion is now a critical problem in American agriculture, then more facts will indicate that it is not as bad as it *could* be and that Iowa will continue to have topsoil for as long as seventy more years. If facts show that some people are undernourished in America, further facts reveal that we should all be glad we do not live in India. This, of course, is machine thought.

To think better, to think like the best humans, we are probably going to have to learn again to judge a person's intelligence, not by the ability to recite facts, but by the good order or harmoniousness of his or her surroundings. We must suspect that any statistical justification of ugliness and violence is a revelation of stupidity. As an earlier student of agriculture put it: "The intelligent man, however unlearned, may be known by his surroundings, and by the care of his horse, if he is fortunate enough to own one."

My second conclusion is that any public program to preserve land or produce food is hopeless if it does not tend to right the balance between numbers of people and acres of land, and to encourage long-term, stable connections between families and small farms. It could be argued that our nation has never made an effort in this direction that was knowledgeable enough or serious enough. It is certain that no such effort, here, has ever succeeded. The typical American farm is probably sold and remade—often as part of a larger farm—at least every generation. Farms that have been passed to the second generation of the same family are unusual. Farms that have passed to the third generation are rare.

But our crying need is for an agriculture in which the typical farm would be farmed by the third generation of the same family. It would be wrong to try to say exactly what kind of agriculture that would be, but it may be allowable to suggest that certain good possibilities would be enhanced.

The most important of those possibilities would be the lengthening of memory. Previous mistakes, failures, and successes would be remembered. The land would not have to pay the cost of a trial-and-error education for every new owner. A half century or more of the farm's history would be living memory, and its present state of health could be measured against its own past—something exceedingly difficult *outside* of living memory.

A second possibility is that the land would not be overworked to pay for itself at full value with every new owner.

A third possibility would be that, having some confidence in family continuity in place, present owners would have future owners not only in supposition but *in sight* and so would take good care of the land, not for the sake of something so abstract as "the future" or "posterity," but out of particular love for living children and grandchildren.

A fourth possibility is that having the past so immediately in memory, and the future so tangibly in prospect, the human establishment on the land would grow more permanent by the practice of better carpentry and masonry. People who remembered long and well would see the folly of rebuilding their barns every generation or two, and of building new fences every twenty years.

A fifth possibility would be the development of the concept of *enough*. Only long memory can answer, for a given farm or locality, How much land is enough? How much work is enough? How much livestock and crop production is enough? How much power is enough?

A sixth possibility is that of local culture. Who could say what that would be? As members of a society based on the exploitation of its own temporariness, we probably should not venture a guess. But we can perhaps speak with a little competence of how it would begin. It would not be imported from critically approved cultures elsewhere. It would not come from watching certified classics on television. It would begin in work and love. People at work in communities three generations old would know that their bodies renewed, time and again, the movements of other bodies, living and dead, known and loved, remembered and loved, in the same shops, houses, and fields. That, of course, is a description of a kind of community dance. And such a dance is perhaps the best way we have to describe harmony.

A mind not to be chang'd by Place or Time.
The mind is its own place, and in itself
Can make a Heav'n of Hell, a Hell of Heav'n.
What matter where, if I be still the same . . .
                    Paradise Lost, I, 253–256

                    .

". . . a post-symbolist enchiridion: the poem as simultaneous
structure, impersonal, autonomous, released from the charge of
expression, of assertion; the poem as arbitrary construct, ab-
surd, self-destroying, no longer aspiring to convince or even to
hoax; the poem as an agent of transformation, equal in value to
the poet himself and therefore capable of changing him; the
poem as means of escape from identity, leading into a world of
contemplation, indifference, bliss."
                    Richard Howard, *Alone with America*, 22

                    .

Bliss is the indispensable goal. But there are orders and obligations this side of bliss. Ignoring these, poetry becomes analogous
to those religious sects that aspire to reach Heaven by faith
alone. The necessity of good works prevents the specialization
of religion. Devotion to order that is not poetical prevents the
specialization of poetry. When the artifact is equal to its maker it

may change him, all right—but willy-nilly and arbitrarily. A poem can be made equal to a poet only by reducing the definition and identity of the poet.

The autonomy of estheticism is a fantasy. It is characteristically an adolescent fantasy. Reality is in the study of dependences.

"Nor am I for a changeless tradition. . . . But those themes we share and inherit, so long as they engage our emotions, come first.

"When that is no longer possible we are broken off and separate . . . and the time has come to read criticism and talk of our point of view.

. . . .

"I say . . . that it is our first business to paint, or describe, desirable people, places, states of mind."

Willam Butler Yeats, *Essays and Introductions*, ix–x (1937)

To be autonomous, in the sense of Howard's definition of post-symbolism, is to be "broken off and separate."

There are obligations to "identity" that must precede an escape from it.

The sense of the placement of an artifact in the world, among other things, in use and among uses, leads directly to considerations of quality and technique. If the builder knows where the house is to be built and who will live in it, and if he respects that place and those people, then he must necessarily strive to build a good house.

The structure of a poem ultimately involves the structure of the life around it.

.

Structure is intelligibility.

.

Ideally, a poem responds to its surroundings, and its surroundings respond to it. Its true growth comes, not from being carried forward in the various stages of a strictly poetic development, but in the interaction of words and deeds. Or the language of poets is the vector that carries vision into and (since no action fully enacts vision) out of action. And action is the vector that carries vision into and out of poems. Without this crisscrossing, vision perishes—just as the sexual impulse perishes (with life itself) if it is not passed continuously back and forth between male and female.

.

That "the poem is . . . equal in value to the poet himself and therefore capable of changing him" is not a reasonable statement. We can be changed by forces either greater or lesser than ourselves. And for better or worse.

.

No product can be the equal of its source. The source is infinite, the product finite.

.

Love poems that are meant as such aspire to the real world, not a word world. They have tried autonomy and found it lonesome; they seek "to form a more perfect union."

.

As an art moves from cultural necessity toward "performance," its materials and concerns increasingly come to be thought of as "subject matter." Making a poem becomes more worthy than to say something to somebody. The poet begins to talk to himself— and to resent the scarcity of eavesdroppers.

.

When performance replaces function, a place becomes a "scene." When Troy and Ithaca are thought of as "scenes" the first great downward step has been taken.

.

The poem and its subject come to be one in the sense that, like lovers, they are clarified and unabashed in each other's presence.

They do not come into each other's presence in the poem, but in the world.

.

Because each work of art exists in the world, in reference to or in relation to all other created things, it can have neither no meaning nor a single, literal meaning. Its meanings resonate and accumulate within and among and in response to the meanings of other things.

.

In the present organization of intelligence—based on the "university" of departmented or encapsulated specialties—the literary understanding elaborates itself within itself, becoming necessarily more and more abstruse. It gets caught in the drift toward "professional" jargon. The only way for this—or any— discipline to advance without becoming more ingrown and purposeless is to take up the question of its relation to other disciplines.

But that calls for a different kind of mind and a different kind of university, in which the motions of intelligence would not follow radii ever outward from the center, each discipline dividing farther from the others the farther outward it goes, but would move in a dance pattern of exchanges and returns. Literary scholars might then begin to teach biology, history, philosophy, science, etc., not to be versatile, but to be pertinent. Writers would begin to feel the judgment of engineers, farmers, and doctors. The immediate benefit would be the death of jargon. In poetry we would see how much of our work depends on shared specialistic assumptions—on the assumption, to begin with, that our "best" if not our only readers will be critics and other poets.

.

The refinement of specialization is analogous to self-absorption and is a kind of crudity. What is wanted in the disciplines is something akin to the refinement of courtesy, each acting out of a sense of the possible conviviality and harmony of all.

.

But if work is to be done well there must be some specialization. The aspect of poetry that is properly special is its technique. The specifically poetic or literary judgment has to do with the quality of workmanship. And yet, even in the consideration of workmanship, judgment must finally refer to things outside poetry— as in considering the proprieties of diction, tone, and rhythm; as in measuring the poem against its subject or reason or occasion.

.

In contemporary writing about poetry there is little concern for either the workmanship or the truth of poems—in comparison, say, to the concern for theme, imagery, impact, the psychology of "creativity"—because there is so little sense of what, or whom, the poems are *for*. When we regain a sense of what poems are for, we will renew the art (the technical means) of writing them. And so we will renew their ability to tell the truth.

.

When a poet takes himself as his subject, he leaves out the issue of propriety altogether. He does not know the difference between what is appropriate and what is interesting, or the difference between what interests him and what interests everybody.

.

The standard of decorum calls all available art and learning and experience into its service; that of "originality," as often construed, calls only for self-importance, irreverence, and recklessness—the "daring" of the manifestoes and reviews.

.

The issue of obedience is obsolete in the modern mind.

.

By taking oneself too seriously one is prevented from being serious enough.

.

If we don't know what poetry is inferior to, we don't know what it is superior to.

.

The notion that a poem is autonomous seems to appropriate the divine characteristic of self-sufficiency—which theology and biology deny to creatures—to apply it to the creature of a creature.

.

Nothing exists for its own sake, but for a harmony greater than itself, which includes it. A work of art, which accepts this condition, and exists upon its terms, honors the Creation, and so becomes a part of it.

.

The right use of any art or discipline leads *out* of it—as the right use of words leads to a heightened awareness both of the referents of words and of the knowledge, feelings, experiences that cannot be expressed or communicated by words.

.

The form of a poem is invisible. A poem is not an "object." This is hard to accept in a mechanical age.

.

It is the thought of not writing poetry down that returns us to its mnemonic (its musical) character.

.

Poetry is an art based on memorability: the memorability of event and insight; the memorability of phrase, sentence, and verse. If the technique of memorability is upheld, it may act as a discriminating threshold, admitting only what is worth remembering. Thus poetry may serve at once to make memorable and to determine what should be remembered.

.

". . . the music of verse is strongest in poetry which has a definite meaning expressed in the properest words."

T. S. Eliot, *On Poetry and Poets*, 183

.

Meaning is destroyed by readers who take one's subject to be one's "image" or one's "subject matter," as if the subject exists only for the poem.

.

We are aware of poetry meandering from the influence of literature to that of "living speech." The best poets have resolved this, of course, by accepting both influences. But if we wish to consider the use or influence of poetry itself, we must think of the possibility that it might influence speech—as, at times, it has.

.

As in manufacturing, the *occasion* of the making of a poem has come to be the availability of raw material, not need.

.

Industrial poetry, like other industrial products, was made possible by an unprecedented displacement of faith and delegation of responsibility. The industrial or specialist poet leaves it to other people to worry about all the practical considerations of his or her connections to the world: food, clothing, shelter, transportation, etc.

.

"Authority has abandoned the task of illuminating the laws of Nature, has forfeited the position of the friendly judge, scarcely now ventures even to adopt the tone of the earnest advocate: it has sunk to the inferior and petty work of photographing the corpse. . . ."

Sir Albert Howard, *The Soil and Health*, p. 81

.

Culture has been reduced to art; art to the works of artists in museums, concert halls, and libraries, which are patronized by non-artists in their leisure time. Thus both culture and art are divorced from work, from the everyday lives of most people, and from action. Culture and art are inactive, received passively in moments of leisure—a collection of consumer products to be used at discretion and then "disposed of" when the world seems to call for action.

Real—that is, living—art and culture, on the other hand, rise from and return to action, the slightest as well as the grandest *deeds* of everybody's everyday life. How much excellence in "the arts" is to be expected from a people who are poor at carpentry, sewing, farming, gardening, and cooking? To believe that you can have a culture distinct from, or as a whole greatly better than, such work is not just illogical or wrong—it is to make peace with the shoddy, the meretricious, and the false.

I have made my motto: No high culture without low culture—which, Gary Snyder says, can also be stated: The lesser truths are also true.

.

I am endlessly in need of the work of poets who have been concerned with living in place, the life of a place, long-term attention and devotion to a settled home and its natural household, and hence to the relation between imagination and language and a place. The work of these poets suggests the possibility that action can again become the subject of poetry. Whether or not we are near to a revival of narrative in poetry, I am not sure. Serious questions lie in the way—not least, questions of propriety. Can, for instance, a serious tale now be told in verse without diluting the verse into prose, or calling undue attention to the verse? But action can only be understood in relation to place; only by staying in place can the imagination conceive or understand action in terms of consequence, of cause and effect. The meaning of action in time is inseparable from its meaning in place.

.

To stay at home is paradoxically to change, to move. When poets—and people of any other calling—stay at home the first thing they move away from is professionalism. They move away from "professional standards." Their work begins to develop under pressure of questions not primarily literary: What good is it? Is it at home here? What do the neighbors think of it? Do they read it, any of them? What have they contributed to it? What does it owe to them?

.

Ken Kesey: "If you've got it all together, what is that all around it?"

That applies to all human structures, explanations, ideas. Any circle we can draw will leave things out. We cannot comprehend what comprehends us. How much "thought" has subsisted upon the infinite human capacity to be wrong about what is not known?

The chief criterion of thought therefore must be propriety—fittingness to our place in the world, in the order of things, and to our relations of dependence and responsibility with other creatures—which would enable humility, restraint, the practice of the virtues.

.

"The Papago sternly holds to the belief that visions do not come to the unworthy. But to the worthy man who shows himself humble there comes a dream. And the dream always contains a song."

Ruth Murray Underhill, *Singing for Power*,
Berkeley, 1968, p. 7

.

Let not sweete Poets praise, whose onely pride
Is vertue to aduaunce, and vice deride,
Be with the works of losels wit defamed,
Ne let such verses Poetrie be named . . .
Spenser, *Mother Hubberds Tale*, 811–814

.

The winged imagination, the imagination free and unfettered, is the specialized imagination. The unspecialized imagination may imagine a farm, a factory, a community, a marriage, a family, a household, a city, a poem—but only as a first step. Having imagined one, it will then strive to imagine the relation of that one to all the rest. It is, thus, a disciplined imagination. It is a formal imagination. It is concerned with relation, dependence, propriety, proportion, balance.

·

The concept of autonomy in poetry seems to alienate the concepts of failure and success. If a thing can succeed only in being what it is, then it cannot fail; in the absence of the possibility of failure, success means nothing.

·

Poetry regards neither nature alone nor humanity alone nor God alone. It is concerned with the order that makes possible the conviviality of the three. It cannot pretend that we live in Paradise or in Hell; by definition, it must be a product of the land eastward of Eden.

·

Reverence makes it possible to be whole, though ignorant. It is the wholeness of understanding.

·

The imagination is our way in to the divine Imagination, permitting us to see wholly—as whole and holy—what we perceive as scattered, as order what we perceive as random.

·

We live in eternity while we live in time. It is only by imagination that we know this.

·

To preserve our places and to be at home in them, it is necessary to fill them with imagination. To imagine as well as see what is in them. Not to fill them with the junk of fantasy and unconsciousness, for that is no more than the industrial economy would do, but to see them first clearly with the eyes, and then to see them with the imagination in their sanctity, as belonging to the Creation.

To imagine the place as it is, and was, and—*only then*—as it will or may be. To imagine its human life only in harmony with its nonhuman life—as one, only one, of its possibilities. In that imagining, perhaps we may begin to see it in its sacredness, as unimaginable gift, as mystery—as it was, is, and ever shall be, world without end.

5

Poetry and Place (1982)

If you ask a Pygmy why his people have no chiefs, no lawgivers, no councils, or no leaders, he will answer with misleading simplicity, "Because we are the people of the forest." The forest, the great provider, is the one standard by which all deeds and thoughts are judged; it is the chief, the lawgiver, the leader, and the final arbitrator.

Colin M. Turnbull, *The Forest People*

A sentence of my own, written thirteen years ago, has stayed in my mind. In it, I was speaking of the connection between my work on the small hill farm where I live and my work as a poet: "This place has become the form of my work, its discipline, in the same way the sonnet has been the form and discipline of the work of other poets: if it doesn't fit it's not true."[1]

This connection between the two kinds of work and between my work and this place has seemed to me both interesting and problematical. And my old statement of it is far too simple. I wrote the sentence because I *felt* it to be true. I still feel that it is, and think so too, but I can no longer feel it or think it so simply. A place can be the form of a poem (or any other work done in it)—and that it should be, I think, is desirable and necessary— but only under certain conditions, and only in a certain sense. I want to return now to attempt to define those conditions and that sense.

I am enabled to do this, not only by my own experience of living, working, and writing in the same place during the intervening thirteen years, but also by news coming to me, through that time, of poets among my contemporaries whose work was being formed in response to a place: John Haines on his Alaska homestead, Gary Snyder in the Sierra foothills, Hayden Carruth in Johnson, Vermont, Donald Hall on his ancestral farm in New Hampshire. I name those particular poets because I have been encouraged by their examples—though, of course, I do not mean to burden them with any responsibility for what I will say, or to imply that they would necessarily agree with me. Their work, or significant parts of it, can be said to be, in the best sense, domestic. And it raises forcibly—as a great deal of contemporary poetry does not—the question of the status of poetry as a reference or response to a subject or a context outside itself.

What I was writing against then, as now, is the poetic principle of "autonomy" or "art for art's sake."

I keep going back to these lines from Auden's elegy, "In Memory of W. B. Yeats":

> . . . poetry makes nothing happen: it survives
> In the valley of its making where executives
> Would never want to tamper . . .

I ask myself if these lines are contradicted by the statement that poetry is "a way of happening, a mouth." But a way for *what* to happen? The last phrase suggests that it is a way only for speech or for poetry itself to happen.

Or are they contradicted by the last lines of the poem:

> In the prison of his days
> Teach the free man how to praise.

But praise *what*? and *why*?

I am not persuaded that the confusion here is all mine. But I am pretty well convinced that when Auden wrote that "poetry makes nothing happen," he believed it, and that, moreover, he was glad to believe it. This conclusion, it seems to me, is supported by other aspects of the poem. By its condescension toward "executives." By its cuteness:

> The death of the poet was kept from his poems.

By its self-conscious and presumptuous modernity:

> The squares of his mind were empty,
> Silence invaded the suburbs,
> The current of his feeling failed . . .

By its wearied and belittling sophistication:

> A few thousand will think of this day
> As one thinks of a day when one did something slightly unusual.

And by its compulsive disparagement and begging off:

> You were silly like us; your gift survived it all . . .

—a line punctuated by two nearly audible sighs of relief: that the poet, being no better than "us," need not trouble us by his example; and that his gift, by presumably surviving his silliness, can be presumed to have been separate from him. This separation of the poet and his gift is the beginning of several kinds of trouble; it is closely akin to Milton's Satan's equally arbitrary and wishful separation of his mind from himself and his predicament:

> The mind is its own place; and in itself
> Can make a Heav'n of Hell, a Hell of Heav'n.[2]

The poem—to use a concept now out of favor, but nevertheless indispensable—lacks decorum. It is not fitting to its subject; it hardly exists even in reference to its subject. It appears to come from the same impulse that keeps translating some great work into slang or "common English" or "the vocabulary of a twelve-year-old." Thus Auden memorializes the death of Yeats in a Modernese that compulsively trivializes it (and him)—and so fails to take Yeats either as seriously or as lightly as he took himself.

To see what I mean, put beside this poem by Auden one by Yeats on essentially the same subject, "The Tower." It is not possible— at least it is not possible for me—to read the last section of that poem without awareness of the influence in it of Yeats's sense of decorum, of his years of arduous study of the proprieties—the technical, the workmanly proprieties—that permit one to speak of great and sacred things:

> . . . being dead, we rise,
> Dream, and so create
> Translunar Paradise.
> I have prepared my peace
> With learned Italian things
> And the proud stones of Greece,
> Poet's imaginings
> And memories of love,
> Memories of the words of women,
> All those things whereof
> Man makes a superhuman
> Mirror-resembling dream.

It is the death of *this* mind that Auden compares to an electrical power failure, as though it had been no more than some industrial gadget.

I do not mean that Auden's poem is not "well made," but only that it is indecorous, unseemly—and flagrantly so. And I think that it is so by a studied, fashionable, even ostentatious indifference to the problem of decorum. Auden wanted to write a doctrinally modernistic elegy, using industrial imagery, the subject being a matter of subordinate importance. The poem, the "art object," is preferred to its subject. It proposes to exist for its own sake.

As this poem sufficiently shows, the connection between the study of decorum and artistic quality is not direct. There is nevertheless a connection that, once broken, will sooner or later prove to have been essential to the maintenance of artistic quality and to the health of artistic discipline as it descends through the generations. This poem, which is technically excellent, belongs in a line of descent that has led to the decay of interest in technique and to the substitution of quantitative for qualitative standards. It has led to a kind of "cheap energy" poetry, a voluminously inflated, mass-produced, journalized product, little used, but nevertheless the basis of a rich commerce in subsidies, grants, and teaching jobs. And it has led to a literary judgment that is little concerned about technique, but is impressionistic, promotional, vague, preoccupied with sensation, "power," "originality," and an endless, idle, boring, trivializing elucidation of "themes." We have a "professional" study of poetry that is useless to everybody but students of poetry, and that a mercenary, job-keeping usefulness; and we have a poetry that is less and less useful to anybody but poets, and its usefulness to them, too often, is also a mercenary, job-keeping usefulness. From reading in magazines, anthologies, and books that come to me, I gather that we now have as a "norm" a mode of poetry that in its slackened rhythms, its resolute ordinariness of diction and subject, its casualness and easiness of form, its rote devices of "originality" and innovation, its uniform of literary rebellion, its formulaic distortions of perception, its conventional mimicries of psychological "depth," its ostentatious or negligent obscurities, its squalid self-revelations, its moral indifference, is a virtual institutionalization of a kind of semi-consciousness. It involves a severely attenuated awareness, most noticeably, of the moral implications of words, thoughts, and acts, and of the consequences of those, both practical and spiritual.

I do not mean that I find no excellences in contemporary poetry. I do find them, but I am afraid that they are *personal* excellences, not residual in a live tradition or in the community of living poets, and therefore extremely vulnerable to time and mortality—in a sense, almost accidental. I am afraid that this "norm" I have described is what we have *instead* of a live tradition; it is what conveys the demands of the art of poetry to the young. And they cannot learn from it that the art demands any self-mastery or any mastery of knowledge or discipline or order or technique. What it apparently suggests as often as not is that poetry demands a willingness to exploit oneself—to display oddities of personality, psychology, or sexuality, or fashionable stigmata of race or gender. And it apparently suggests that this data need be illuminated by no insight or form, that it may be arranged arbitrarily in "lines" of which the rhythms vary flaccidly from excited to somnolent, and that so to present it is "powerful" and "courageous."

But if it is concluded that "poetry makes nothing happen," such an inflation and degradation of poetry is to be expected. The very center of Auden's poem—and of its fault—is his disdainful separation of the making of poetry from the interests of "executives." I assume that Auden used "executives" more or less as a synonym for "businessmen," but his choice of the word is nevertheless significant, for an "executive," literally, is one who executes, acts, "puts into effect." Once the connection between words and acts, words and things, poems and effects is broken, once poems assume that they will and can "make nothing happen," then they must perforce strive for "autonomy"; they must propose to exist "for their own sake." But this would make them anomalous, unique in all creation. What else exists for its own sake? What else would want to? Or to put it less affectively, what, having had a cause, can in the nature of things avoid becoming itself a cause? How, once a thing exists, can it be prevented from having an effect? How, once its inevitable power as a cause is granted, can its effect avoid being either bad or good? And how, if there is no conscious effort to make it good, can it avoid being bad?

A product that exists for its own sake is a debased *and a debasing* product. And it is a kind of product that did not exist before the "consumer economy" made useless "goods" a part of everyday experience. But of course nothing human exists without a human purpose somewhere back of it and a human effect somewhere ahead of it. If things are made for no good purpose, are made to *serve* no good purpose, then they corrupt their causes, and they have bad effects. "Autonomous" poems, I think, *do* make something happen, and are so intended: they accredit their makers as "poets"—the worst possible reason for poetry to exist. They thus corrupt the "poet" by allowing him or her to fulfill too easily a dangerous ambition. And they corrupt poetry, language, and the art of reading by offering the reader words that avoid any purpose or reference—and, sooner or later, also any poetic tradition—by which their truth or excellence can be measured. We wind up with a product not made in any line of descent of the art of poetry, but one made in helpless imitation of the "consumer products" of a "cheap energy" industrial economy. We wind up with poems which, in value and justification, do not differ greatly from chewing gum.

Where does this state of poetry stand us in looking at the great poets of the past? It obviously must greatly diminish their influence, since their poems—unless we count the fairly recent past—are not "autonomous" and cannot be understood on the assumption that they are. But it also makes it difficult for us to see and appreciate what it means that their poems were *not meant* to be "autonomous."

I believe that at the source of our poetry is the idea that poetry must be used for something, must serve something, greater and higher than itself. It is a way to learn, know, celebrate, and remember the truth—or, as Yeats said, to "Bring the soul of man to God."[3] And Yeats was never less "silly" or eccentric than when he said that; he was speaking out of the traditional mainstream.

To Dante, *The Divine Comedy* is not his ambition, much less an "art object"—it is a blessing and a trial, a privilege and an obligation. By his merit as man and poet, but also necessarily by

God's will and grace, he attains a vision of the truth, which then, by virtue of his poetic merit, he is under obligation to *tell*, so that, as the Apostle James says to him, "you may strengthen in yourself and others the Hope which there below rightly enamors. . . ."[4] There is no denying Dante's ambition to be a great poet; there was, as he acknowledges, a heavy dross of pride in him. But we must be careful, for with these old poets there is always a sense in which their desire for fame is a desire, not to be "famous" as we understand that word, but to be *worthy*—a sense in which the desire to be a great poet follows logically from the attempt on, the gift of, a great subject. It is an ambition required by *humility*; what a damning presumption it would be to write less than greatly on a great subject! How blasphemous to be *willing* to do so!

The same understanding applies to Milton, who in "Lycidas" defines poetic ambition (desire for "fame") in two almost opposite senses. In the first, "fame" is a good worldly reputation which, if earned and deserved, is of some value, though its value is limited and subject to chance and mortality. The other sense is absolute, and has to do not with "reputation" but with worthiness:

> *Fame* is no plant that grows on mortal soil,
> Nor in the glistering foil
> Set off to th' world, nor in broad rumor lies,
> But lives and spreads aloft by those pure eyes
> And perfect witness of all-judging *Jove*;
> As he pronounces lastly on each deed,
> Of so much fame in Heav'n expect thy meed.[5]

Here as elsewhere, Milton was obviously thinking of the Parable of the Talents and of his own "one talent" with which he felt himself obliged to serve "my Maker."[6] Whatever desire for worldly fame was in him, he understood himself as working not in the world's eyes, but "in my great Task-Master's eye."[7] He returns to this again in *Paradise Regained*:

This is true glory and renown, when God
Looking on th' Earth, with approbation marks
The just man . . .[8]

And this understanding—with one momentous breach—governs the invocations of *Paradise Lost*.

Once the poem is understood as serving a truth outside and greater than itself, the poet serves the poem with his or her whole life, not just with "talent," observation, ideas, verbal gifts, and so on. "So that how he should be truly eloquent who is not withall a good man, I see not," Milton said.[9] And he held that "he who would not be frustrate of his hope to write well hereafter in laudable things ought him selfe to bee a true Poem, that is, a composition, and patterne of the best and honourablest things; not presuming to sing high praises of heroick men, or famous Cities unlesse he have in himselfe the experience and the practice of all that which is praise-worthy."[10] And in *Comus* he wrote that "none / But such as are good men can give good things. . . ."[11] Milton, of course, did not perfectly live up to his ideal—a failure for which I think that he has been too specially indicted—but no ideal is invalidated by anyone's, or by everyone's, failure to live fully up to it, and here we are not so much concerned to judge the lives of poets as to understand the values and assumptions that support the writing of the best poems.

In Dante more than in Milton we see the poetry served by the whole life of the poet—not a life "dedicated to poetry," or a life exploited for "subject matter," but a life lived in devotion to "the Love which moves the sun and the other stars,"[12] and in the Hope "which divine grace produces, and preceding merit."[13] To attempt, with Robert Lowell, to understand Dante on the reductive modernist assumption that he was "silly like us" ("Where, where, in the whole *Commedia*, are Mrs. Dante and the Dante children?")[14] may be right or wrong about Dante, but it is certainly to be wrong about his values and his poem. Dante, being human, partook of "our" silliness. So we must assume. But what would it mean if we proved that he did, or if he had so proved by confession? We would still have to reckon with his power to exalt his humanity and ours far above silliness.

So far, I have considered poetry's service to truth as a spiritual and an ethical matter, and this service does begin and end with such concerns. But insofar as it is performed by poetry and not another kind of work, such service raises ultimately the whole array of technical questions, and it raises them more urgently, I believe, than they can otherwise be raised. It does this by the questions having to do with propriety or decorum: What is the kind, quality, and importance of the subject? What, then, would be the appropriate or fitting or seemly form, style, diction, rhythm with which to treat it? When the poet believes that his poem is about, or in service to, a subject greater than itself (and than him- or herself), these questions become paramount.

In his essay "Of Education," Milton speaks of the need to teach "those organic arts which inable men to discourse and write perspicuously, elegantly, and according to the fitted stile of lofty, mean, or lowly." This is the "due place" of logic and rhetoric, but "precedent" to those would be the study of poetry: "I mean not here the prosody of a verse . . . but that sublime Art which . . . teaches . . . what the laws are of a true *Epic* poem, what of a *Dramatic*, what of a *Lyric*, *what Decorum is, which is the grand master-piece to observe* [my emphasis]. This would . . . show them what religious, what glorious and magnificent use might be made of poetry, both in divine and human things."[15] This, in its belief that poetry serves both reader and subject, is antithetical to any idea of the "autonomy" of poetry, but I have quoted it mainly to display the importance he gives to the understanding—hence, to the practice—of decorum.

Milton cites Aristotle's *Poetics* here, and the concern for decorum certainly goes farther back—to the belief among the poets read by Aristotle that one should "say such things as are true and proper. . . ."[16] But a more useful understanding of the value and function of decorum is given in Milton's poetry. In the early poem, "At a Vacation Exercise in the College," addressing his "native language," he seems to be saying that—given a proper respect for himself, his language, and his art—he cannot speak at all without due consideration of decorum:

> I have some naked thoughts that rove about,
> And loudly knock to have their passage out,
> And weary of their place do only stay
> Till thou hast deck't them in thy best array . . .

And then, characteristically recalling his aspiration "that with no middle flight intends to soar," he says:

> Yet had I rather, if I were to choose,
> Thy service in some graver subject use,
> Such as may make thee search thy coffers round,
> Before thou clothe my fancy in fit sound . . .[17]

One may perhaps see a youthful simplicity in the rather mechanical concept of language as the clothes of thought or imagination, but not, I think, in the understanding that there should be a fittingness of sound to subject. This has come to maturity in the invocation to "holy Light" at the beginning of Book III of *Paradise Lost*, when the poet prays: "May I express thee unblam'd?"[18] Here he is still aspiring, but humbled in *and by* his aspiration, realizing as he comes face to face with it that the "graver" the subject the graver the moral and spiritual peril. And so he prays to be enabled to speak decorously, both appropriately and truly, and here the propriety and the truth of words, the seeing and the telling, have become one:

> . . . Celestial Light,
> Shine inward, and the mind through all her powers
> Irradiate, there plant eyes; all mist from thence
> Purge and disperse, that I may see and tell
> Of things invisible to mortal sight.[19]

But in asking to "see . . . things invisible," these lines also provide the key to what I believe is the great flaw of *Paradise Lost*, and it is a flaw made in a violation of decorum. Humbled and even daunted as he is by the height and difficulty of his aspiration, his very prayer transforms it into ambition, a kind of artistic hubris. He prays, not that his desire should be proper, but simply that it should be fulfilled, and what he desires is both excessive and self-defeating, for it is insolubly paradoxical: a mortal cannot see "things invisible to mortal sight." His prayer, it seems to me, was not granted.

One of the larger concerns of decorum, reaching to more than literature, is the question of what is proper to *do*. But the question of the propriety of action is unanswerable by itself. It cannot be answered, or even intelligibly asked, except in terms of the question of propriety of place—not just of the immediate human and worldly context of the action, but of the place of the actor in the order of Creation. How you act *should* be determined, and the consequences of your acts *are* determined, by where you are. To know where you are (and whether or not that is where you should be) is at least as important as to know what you are doing, because in the moral (the ecological) sense you cannot know *what* until you have learned *where*. Not knowing where you are, you can make mistakes of the utmost seriousness: you can lose your soul or your soil, your life or your way home.

But minds of our century must take care to understand that, for the old poets, the question of the whereabouts of an action was not just social and geographical; it was hierarchical. It was, so to speak, both horizontal and vertical. Any action raised questions about proprieties of place, time, manners, comportment, style; but it also raised questions of *value*. An act might be appropriate for a human being of a given quality, or it might be degrading (vulgar or bestial) or arrogant. It might violate local conditions or mores, or it might usurp divine prerogative. In the story of Moses and the burning bush we see the crossing of these two axes in such a way as to define Moses' whereabouts with the gravest exactitude. The voice from the bush gives him his worldly location: "the place whereon thou standest is holy ground"— but not until it has placed him properly in the hierarchical order (he is merely a man): "put off thy shoes from off thy feet. . . ."[20]

Before the specialization of the disciplines that accompanied the Industrial Revolution, one of the dominant strains of Western culture was a concern for the limits of responsible action. And these limits were defined primarily by the human place, below the angels and above the animals, in the hierarchy of created things. To act in violation of these limits is to invite consequences that cannot be controlled, and may not be survived.

Paradise Lost is written in praise of this hierarchical order, which Satan violates by pride and then causes Eve to violate by pride. In Dante this pride is understood as impatience, unwillingness to wait for the light,[21] which is a good enough characterization of the pride of Satan and Eve in *Paradise Lost*—but it is the *literal* description of Milton's pride in the invocation of Book III. Milton's pride was not satanic, except insofar as *all* pride may be; it seems to have been somehow inadvertent as if coming from his personality, which Dr. Johnson understood as disobedient or unruly ("he hated all whom he was required to obey"),[22] and not his will. So far as his will and understanding went, he condemned this sort of pride and condemns it explicitly in *Paradise Lost*, Book VIII, when, replying to Adam's question about "celestial Motions," Raphael says:

> Solicit not thy thoughts with matters hid . . .
> . . . .
>   Heav'n is for thee too high
> To know what passes there; be lowly wise:
> Think only what concerns thee and thy being;
> Dream not of other Worlds . . .[23]

And Milton even says of himself, with exact insight, in the invocation of Book VII: "More safe I sing with mortal voice. . . ."[24] And here he seems relieved that the remainder of his poem will be sung "Standing on Earth."[25]

Even so, he allowed his artistic pride to carry his inward vision or imagination directly into Heaven, and so was forced to bring

God on stage *in person*, not as inscrutable mystery and power, visible blindingly, but as a heroic king conversing in Homeric dialogue with the Son. I have no inclination to condemn these passages; they are essential to the poem, are in most ways worthy of it, and contain some magnificent verse. But they are not believable. The more we hear about what God does and says, the more incredible He becomes. You cannot "see the unseen" without making it visible, and you cannot make it visible without making it less—not, perhaps, less majestic or less sublime, but less mysterious and less awesome. I am not talking about the difference between mystery and revelation but, rather, the difference between the suffering incarnate Christ and Christ in the *character* of omnipotent deity, or the difference between God as represented by a spokesman or present as a voice in the Old Testament and the voluble discourser in *Paradise Lost*. The *revealed* God of the Bible is never more than partially revealed and is therefore not reduced to the scale or the comprehension of the mortals to whom He is revealing Himself. But when the "Almighty Father" of *Paradise Lost*, Book III, addresses His other Person, improbably, as "Only begotten Son" and proceeds to tell Him a great deal that in His omniscience He must already know, He seems to speak in imitation of those false dramatic lines meant only to inform the audience, and the lines are overpowered by our awareness that they helplessly reduce what they seek to present. Similarly, when omnipotence is armed with "Bow and Quiver," or even with "three-bolted Thunder," it must seem less than omnipotent. The difference is that between revelation and presentation. Aspiring to "see" the one God of Abraham, Isaac, and Jacob, Milton falls onto Olympus.[26] If here he "wrote in fetters when he wrote of Angels & God"[27] it was because he did not recognize his problem as a problem of decorum, and so tried to solve it by a kind of assault. If he was "of the Devil's party without knowing it"[28]—as in this particular respect I think he may have been—it was for the same reason: not because he was a true poet, but because he was a flawed one. It is by misunderstanding this same problem that Shelley could think Satan the hero of *Paradise Lost*.[29]

Dante, on the other hand, understood the problem for what it was and understood it in both its moral and its artistic aspects. As a result, the decorum of the *Paradiso* is indeed a "grand masterpiece to observe." Hugh MacDiarmid suggested that Dante is the "subject" of his poem as modern poets have made themselves the subject of theirs.[30] But Dante does not write about himself in anything like the way Byron and Wordsworth or Lowell and Sexton write about themselves. He appears in his poem as one of its characters—more prominently than Chaucer appears in *The Canterbury Tales*, but in about the same manner. *The Divine Comedy* is the story of what he experienced on his "pilgrimage." This pilgrimage is not his "life story." To come to this poem inquiring about the author's wife and children is merely pointless.

The great *artistic* significance of Dante's presence in the *Paradiso* is that it requires him to speak in the first person, and in his scrupulous observance of that convention and its implications he solved the problem of decorum. Milton, speaking in sublime "omniscience," reduces omnipotence to a matter of chariots and weapons. Dante, speaking only as himself "with mortal voice," and in a style conscientiously "humble," arduously and by grace ascends to a vision of the Light Supreme, before which his speech fails, of which he can remember only the "sweetness"[31] —but the awesomeness and power of which are borne into the imaginative life of the poem by the very *failure* of speech and memory. The triumph of the poem, finally, is that the unspeakable is *rendered*—made credible, made somehow imaginable— by speechlessness, by the inability to present what has been revealed.

The *Paradiso* is not "about" God any more than it is "about" Dante. Dante's understanding of this is perhaps the essential ground of his propriety. One should not, indeed cannot, focus attention on oneself in the presence of God. On the other hand, a mortal man cannot look so closely or particularly or knowingly at that Light as to presume to say a great deal about it. Glibness would be ruin. To see too much, to say too much, would be as destructive of the dignity of the poem, and of belief in it, as to see and say too little.

And so the poem is "about" contemplation; it is an account of the way the mind ascends by the "ladder" of contemplation to a Truth that can only reveal itself by proving itself finally beyond scrutiny. As a poem about contemplation, the *Paradiso* is free to turn again and again, at each ascending rung of the "ladder," to the question of how much of the light a man can see, how much of his darkness can be lifted. This question and the successive stages of its answer make the drama of the poem. And this drama, this suspense, is always at one level a drama of decorum: Can the poet go higher, can he say more, and be believed? Can he so empower and so restrain this mortal voice, so maintain its intense propriety, as to further exalt it?

The paradox of the poem is that this ascent that exalts the mind defines the mind's limits the more forcibly the higher it rises—toward "a light so keen that the eye on which it blazes needs must close."[32] And the end reached in Canto XXXIII is no ultimate or absolute vision but simply the limit of the pilgrim's mortal power to see. What this ascent does is force the human limit or definition out of the abstracting intellect—where it is a theoretical, arbitrary, and conventional *idea*—into the imagination, giving it the authenticity and the authority of experience.

There are many instances of this in the poem, but none, I think, more startling than when, having come to the song of the light that is the soul of St. Peter, the poet's pen leaps off the page: "a song so divine that my phantasy does not repeat it to me; wherefore my pen leaps and I do not write it. . . ."[33] In that leap of his pen Dante's limitation as a mortal man is caught up quick and bright into his imagination. Decorum ceases to be a peripheral quality or condition of the poem and enters it as a part of its substance.

The limitation is, of course, a Christian one, and in Dante it simply is accepted; it is profoundly understood and approved. He never makes the Miltonic presumption. Milton's passages on Heaven are a poetry of visualization, triumphant in a sense, but in their very triumph defeated; Dante's are a poetry of triumphant *faith*, which always implies the necessary failure of visualization. This failure belongs to the Christian definition of humanity, and the meticulousness of Dante's observance of it can be extremely moving. In Canto XXV, for example, after he has been examined by St. James on the virtue of Hope, Dante loses his sight because he has tried to *see* what he hopes for (the resurrected body of St. John). This is exactly in keeping with Romans 8:24,25: "For we are saved by hope: but hope that is seen is not hope: for what a man seeth, why doth he yet hope for? But if we hope for that we see not, then do we with patience wait for it." This patience is the difference between Milton's vision of Heaven and Dante's. Dante's is an *humbling* ascension. For him, one can almost say, it is Purgatory all the way through Paradise: every upward step carries him against the gravity of his pride. Milton is a blind man soaring into the sublimity of his "inward" sight; Dante a sighted man, seeing by faith and grace within the limits of his innate blindness. In Dante, vision does rise to heights before unattempted and afterwards unsurpassed, but the unseen grows ever greater as vision ascends toward it. The longer the radius of vision, the wider the circumference of mystery.

His vision again failing at the Light, at the beginning of Canto XXX, blindness and love turn him back toward Beatrice, whom he can see but cannot describe. And he now realizes that her beauty is so great that "He alone who made it can enjoy it all." And he must acknowledge himself the most defeated of poets.[34] This is not false humility. Though he is at the summit of poetic vision and accomplishment, he *is* defeated; he has come to his utmost reach, and now, after nearly a lifetime, his song of praise of Beatrice must end. Her beauty is greater than his praise, as it should and must be, as he is glad for it to be. And yet this valediction is a stroke of intense pain—a mortal pain in Heaven, in part the result of a strict decorum, the *honesty* of decorum. And, to me, it is more moving than all of Milton's war of angels. This defeat of Dante's is his triumph—to earn it he had to reach, recognize, and accept failure. And this triumphant defeat is impossible, both inconceivable and unrecognizable, in the terms of 'autonomous' poetry.

Dante's poem both is and is about an act of obedience: the journey to God and all that that implies for a mortal human being. It is everywhere informed, therefore, by an exquisite decorum, both of action and of expression.

Milton's poem, which might be said to have the same general aspiration, and which similarly ascends to Heaven after first descending to Hell, has the opposite subject: disobedience. Whereas Dante is concerned with disobedience only initially and incidentally, Milton seems intensely, compulsively focused upon it, not just consciously but, as Blake says, unconsciously too—not only involved with it by imagination and sympathy, and by human nature, but somehow joined to it, despite his high character, at the unexamined roots of his personality. The artistic arrogance or disobedience of the passages on Heaven is balanced and redeemed by the discourse of Raphael in Book VIII. But it is not cancelled or atoned for; a conscious humility can hardly cancel or atone for an unconscious arrogance, and it seems to me, finally, that the ambitiously soaring poet of the passages on Heaven has thrown a rather portentous shadow on the world.

Between Dante and Milton a profound change occurred that was not merely a difference between two men. A key to understanding this change may be found in *Macbeth*, I, vii. This scene is a reenactment of the temptation of Genesis 3: 1–6 and has the same theme: the desire to behave *inordinately*. Both temptations have to do with the taking by humans of a power that humans cannot properly possess or safely use. In Shakespeare's scene, Macbeth, having made the plan to murder Duncan, has begun to lose his resolve:

> We will proceed no further in this business.
> He hath honored me of late . . .[35]

Whereupon Lady Macbeth speaks, among others, these lines:

> Art thou afeard
> To be the same in thine own act and valor
> As thou art in desire?[36]

And Macbeth, not yet persuaded, replies as Dante might have replied, out of the moral mainstream of his culture:

> I dare do all that may become a man.
> Who dares do more is none.[37]

Probably no literate playgoer of Shakespeare's time could have heard those lines without some awareness of the centuries of thought that had been devoted to the question of what acts were humanly becoming. The scene ends, of course, with the renewal of Macbeth's determination. He kills Duncan and in that act kills law, civility, kindness—all that makes life humanly livable —and sets up in their place the naked force of his ambition. The irony is that such power as he takes cannot be held; in taking it he simply lets it out of control. With Duncan's murder, Macbeth's mind becomes a Hell and for a while it makes a Hell of Scotland.

What happens in scene vii of Act I is the same thing that happens in Genesis 3:1–6. The hierarchical order of Creation, the Chain of Being, is broken; humans have usurped powers that belong only to God; and the consequences are therefore neither foreseeable nor controllable.

The antithetical theme—the antidote—is spoken by Macduff in the third scene of Act IV:

> Boundless intemperance
> In nature is a tyranny.[38]

In such allusions to the doctrine of temperance in the old poets there is at work what I think can justly be called an ecological intelligence: a sense of the impossibility of acting or living alone or solely in one's own behalf, and this rests in turn upon a sense of the order upon which any life depends and of the proprieties of place within that order. Without this intelligence, temperance can govern no act for it cannot be defined. As Macduff speaks of it, temperance is no abstract or ideal virtue, but the enactment, the practice, of the understanding that one lives within an order of dependence and obligation superior to oneself. It is the practice of decorum.

Milton makes this ecological intelligence explicit in *Comus* in an exchange between the Lady and her would-be seducer. Comus speaks in the tradition of *carpe diem*, but makes in the process a prototype of the modern exploiter's argument:

> If all the world
> Should in a pet of temperance feed on Pulse,
> Drink the clear stream, and nothing wear but Frieze,
> Th'all-giver would be unthank't, would be unprais'd,
> Not half his riches known, and yet despis'd,
> And we should serve him as a grudging master,
> As a penurious niggard of his wealth,
> And live like Nature's bastards, not her sons,
> Who would be quite surcharg'd with her own weight,
> And strangl'd with her waste fertility . . .[39]

We recognize this as, among other things, the assumption fundamental to the industrial economy: all that has no human use is "waste." To this the Lady, with fine contemptuous eloquence, replies:

> Impostor, do not charge most innocent nature,
> As if she would her children should be riotous
> With her abundance; she, good cateress,
> Means her provision only to the good
> That live according to her sober laws
> And holy dictate of spare Temperance:
> If every just man that now pines with want

Had but a moderate and beseeming share
Of that which lewdly-pamper'd Luxury
Now heaps upon some few with vast excess,
Nature's full blessings would be well dispens't
In unsuperfluous even proportion,
And she no whit encumber'd with her store,
And then the giver would be better thank't,
His praise due paid, for swinish gluttony
Ne'er looks to Heav'n amidst his gorgeous feast,
But with besotted base ingratitude
Crams, and blasphemes his feeder.[40]

And that is a prototype of the ecological argument of our own time—or it is the traditional morality that we now begin to perceive as ecological: humans can have a decent, permanent place in the earthly household only by knowing precisely the extent of their "beseeming share" and by using no more.[41] One of the rarities of *Comus* is that it is a poem in praise of "the sage / And serious doctrine of Virginity." But this praise does not originate in the prudishness that we would now call "puritanical"; it rises, instead, both from the inherited ancient reverence for the "holy dictate of spare Temperance" and from Milton's own noble preoccupation with the question of the proper use of gifts— gifts, that is, that are not human in origin. *Comus* is misread by those who see in it a simple conflict between chastity and fecundity or temperance and abundance; that is the way Comus himself would read it. The real defender of fecundity and abundance is the Lady. Temperance, not gluttony, is the safeguard of abundance; sexual discipline, not promiscuity, safeguards fecundity.

The Lady of *Comus* is the triumphant counterpart of Eve. Her obedience to "holy dictate" undoes Eve's disobedience. But the temptation scene of *Paradise Lost*, Book IX, greatly enlarges the moral context of the problem of obedience—as well as the moral drama—and gives a better sense of what Milton understood by obedience. From the Lady of *Comus* we understand that obedience is moderate and seemly or decorous behavior within nature. In *Paradise Lost* we understand that the meaning of obedience rests upon natural order, and that the natural order in one of its aspects is moral and hierarchical: the Chain of Being. To obey is to remain steadfastly in the human place in the Chain of Being—that is, to stay within the human definition, "all that may become a man." To disobey is to break out of the human place in the order of Creation. Satan fell because of inordinate desire: he wanted to be God; he wanted no superior in Heaven. And he seduces Eve to analogous disobedience; she too (though "last and best / Of all God's Works")[42] is persuaded that God is a "great Forbidder"[43] and that it would be well to "grow mature / In knowledge, as the Gods who all things know. . . ."[44] Satan's speech to Eve alludes explicitly to the Chain of Being, the order in which he suggests that she is unjustly imprisoned:

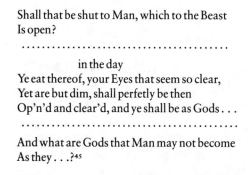

> Shall that be shut to Man, which to the Beast
> Is open?
>
> . . . .
>
>   in the day
> Ye eat thereof, your Eyes that seem so clear,
> Yet are but dim, shall perfetly be then
> Op'n'd and clear'd, and ye shall be as Gods . . .
>
> . . . .
>
> And what are Gods that Man may not become
> As they . . .?[45]

Ambition aspires to godliness, but the mention of "the Beast" is ominous. For apparently one can break out of the human place in only one direction. To move beyond the human toward the godly is only to move toward the bestial: "Who dares do more, is none." Or as Blake puts it: "Attempting to be more than Man we become less. . . ."[46]

As Milton apparently saw it, then, sin or disobedience involves a failure to perceive a contradiction in terms: one sins by assuming that order can accommodate or satisfy inordinate desire. This paradoxical assumption is fundamental to Satan's character; it is why he is such a liar. Because it is alien to the characters of Adam and Eve, it becomes their violation and their tragedy.

It is essential to the meaning of *Paradise Lost*—as to Biblical tradition—that the Fall is not absolute: Adam and Eve fall into sin and death, but not into damnation. And this, in Milton's version of the story, is because Eve experiences one temptation to which she does not succumb—the temptation to be superior to Adam:

> . . . shall I to him make known
> As yet my change, and give him to partake
> Full happiness with mee, or rather not,
> But keep the odds of Knowledge in my power
> Without Copartner? so to add what wants
> In Female Sex, the more to draw his Love,
> And render me more equal, and perhaps,
> A thing not undesirable, sometime
> Superior: for inferior who is free?[47]

But this superiority, as she quickly realizes, is both risky and virtually synonymous with loneliness. She decides to share her fate with Adam and so assures that they will become sinful and mortal, but not hellish.

Perhaps the most significant thing in this passage, so far as the history of culture is concerned, is the fleeting equation of superiority—of *intellectual* superiority—with freedom. Understanding that this equation would destroy the ancient structure of values that he was attempting to defend, Milton causes Eve to reject it as soon as she has thought of it. But the point is that, by Milton's time, it had become possible to imagine—perhaps impossible *not* to imagine—a mind to which this equation would be a creed, for Eve's rejection is but the countermovement to Satan's boast in Book I that "the mind is its own place. . . ."

As it has developed from an imagined possibility in Milton's time to the romantic rebellion of the nineteenth century to the commonplace of self-centeredness that it has become by now, this mind has shaped itself less on the wish rejected by Eve than on the desperate boast of Satan: though it has sometimes made a cause and a shibboleth of human "equality," it has consistently asserted its superiority to its circumstances, whether of the human condition or the natural world. It is the mind that, as Gurney Norman says, "believes there *is* no context until *it* gets there." In one of its aspects, this is the mind of the exploiters of the "unknown," from Cortes and Pizarro down to the scientists of nuclear energy, genetic engineering, space conquest, and war in our own day. In another of its aspects, it is the romantic puritanism of Shelley. And these aspects are not so far apart as one might believe.

In *Paradise Lost*, then, there is a conflict, never acknowledged or resolved and so undoubtedly not conscious, between Milton's own ambition as a theological poet and the traditional concept of the human place in the order of Creation, which he defends in Raphael's discourse in Book VIII and in his narration of the Fall. He apparently never saw the parallel between his prayer to "see and tell / of things invisible to mortal sight" in the invocation of Book III and Satan's proposal to Eve in Book IX that "your Eyes that seem so clear, / Yet are but dim, shall perfetly be then / Op'n'd and Cleared, and ye shall be as Gods. . . ." It even seems that the governing intention of the poem to "justify the ways of God to men" is seriously embarrassed if not invalidated by Raphael's instruction in Book VIII:

> Heav'n is for thee too high
> To know what passes there, be lowly wise:
> Think only what concerns thee and thy being;
> Dream not of other Worlds . . .[48]

That is to say that by the poem's most traditional terms, theodicy is a kind of *hubris* or a kind of blasphemy.

This conflict between the aspiring individual mind and the traditional idea of universal order is concurrent with the English Reformation and Revolution, in both of which Milton participated actively as writer and public servant. That his great poem should deal with the archetypal story of such a conflict has therefore a sort of inevitability that is both historical and biographical. That this poem should have as an unconscious theme the conflict between Milton himself and the traditional idea of order may be equally inevitable, but it is much harder to deal with. Both the poem and its poet are too complicated and too deeply involved in problems that still beset us to permit us to indulge in simple explanations. But this unconsciousness of Milton's may be explainable in part by the kind of poem he was writing. A mind strong enough to write *Paradise Lost* at the time and in the circumstances in which Milton wrote it would probably be too strong, too imperiously confident of its own rightness, to notice its own transgressions against the idea of order it had undertaken to defend. And for Milton to have become consciously preoccupied with this personal conflict and the problem of worldly authority that it raises would probably have destroyed his poem. The poem's very nature as a theological epic seems to prohibit attention to this sort of problem, which would bring into question the authority of its own voice. To deal with this problem would require a less confident tone as well as a more deliberative and discriminating kind of verse, "fittest for Discourse, and nearest Prose."

For Dryden, the problem became a conscious crisis of authority and allegiance, a theme at once literary and urgently personal. The first of his poems on this subject was *Religio Laici* which, as Martin Price says,

> tries to create a rational order in the face of reason's limitations. What Dryden seeks to do is defend a religion that can make do without infallibility. He goes about systematically disarming the Deist's trust in the absolute rightness of human reason, the Catholic's trust in the Church as infallible interpreter of revealed truth, and the Dissenter's trust in the infallibility of the individual conscience guided by Scripture.[49]

Dryden sees the Reformation as the result of "a knowing Age" that divides two kinds of religion, equally bad. The first was the spiritual monopoly of the Roman Catholic priesthood:

> When want of Learning kept the *Laymen* low,
> And none but *Priests* were *Authoriz'd* to *know* . . .
> . . . .
> Then *Mother Church* did mightily prevail:
> She parcel'd out the Bible by *retail* . . .[50]

The spread of literacy brought on a new kind of religion with the opposite problem:

> The Book thus put in every vulgar hand,
> Which each presum'd he best cou'd understand,
> The *Common Rule* was made the *common Prey*;
> And at the mercy of the *Rabble* lay.
> The tender Page with horney Fists was gaul'd;
> And he was gifted most that loudest baul'd . . .[51]

Dryden's solution here, though temporary, is to avoid the extremes both of pride and of ignorance:

> Neither so rich a Treasure to forgo;
> Nor proudly seek beyond our pow'r to know:
> Faith is not built on disquisitions vain;
> The things we *must* believe, are *few*, and *plain* . . .
> . . . .
> 'Tis some Relief, that points not clearly known,
> Without much hazard may be let alone . . .
> . . . .
> For points obscure are of small use to learn:
> But *Common quiet* is *Mankind's concern*.[52]

And this rests on a carefully qualified trust in the Bible:

> the *Scriptures*, though not *every where*
> Free from Corruption, or intire, or clear,
> Are uncorrupt, sufficient, clear, intire,
> In *all* things which our needfull *Faith* require.[53]

This is judicious, graceful, eminently sane, and in its moderation it is deeply traditional. Dryden's respect for the limits of our power, and our need, to know recalls Raphael's charge to Adam to be "lowly wise."

But this is a "layman" speaking, not an angel. And as Dryden is careful to insist, he is speaking *for himself*:

> If *others* in the *same Glass better* see
> 'Tis for *Themselves* they look, but not for *me*:
> For *MY* Salvation must its Doom receive
> Not from what *OTHERS*, but what *I* believe.[54]

However scrupulous and responsible, this care to say that this or that is true *for me*, not only leaves the question of authority unsolved, but is a way of stepping around it. To separate faith from "disquisitions" may require acceptance of the impossibility of a solution that is more than personal. And yet to decide what "we *must* believe" and what "can be let alone," to determine "all things *needfull* to be known,"[55] may be intolerable as a personal task, a burden that the individual mind will prove unable to bear alone.

That this was so for Dryden is suggested by *The Hind and the Panther*, in which Dryden defends his conversion to Catholicism. Early in the poem he states the problem rising from the conclusion of *Religio Laici*:

> What weight of antient witness can prevail
> If private reason hold the publick scale?[56]

And this personal problem becomes a public or institutional one. The Anglican church is weak and indecisive because it cannot limit the principle established by its own rebellion:

> Fierce to her foes, yet fears her force to try,
> Because she wants innate auctority;
> For how can she constrain them to obey
> Who has herself cast off the lawfull sway?

. . . .

As long as words a diff'rent sense will bear,
And each may be his own Interpreter,
Our ai'ry faith will no foundation find:
The word's a weathercock for ev'ry wind . . .

. . . .

So hardly can Usurpers manage well
Those, whom they first instructed to rebell . . .[57]

The solution that Dryden proposes is affirmation of Christian tradition as established in the Catholic Church:

The good old Bishops took a simpler way,
Each ask'd but what he heard his Father say,
Or how he was instructed in his youth,
And by traditions force upheld the truth.[58]

These lines are not so simpleminded as they look in isolation, for they answer a problem of extreme difficulty, ably understood:

They try'd the Scripture by tradition's force;
But you [the Anglican Panther] tradition by the Scripture try;
Pursu'd, by Sects, from this to that you fly,
Nor dare on one foundation to rely.
The word is then depos'd, and in this view,
You rule the Scripture, not the Scripture you.

. . . .

I see tradition then is disallow'd,
When not evinc'd by Scripture to be true,
And Scripture, as interpreted by you.
But here you tread upon unfaithfull ground;
Unless you cou'd infallibly expound.
Which you reject as odious Popery . . .[59]

And so Dryden settles at last on one of the possibilities rejected in *Religio Laici*:

It then remains that church can onely be
The guide, which owns unfailing certainty . . .[60]

These two poems bear witness to a painful, difficult, honest struggle. The argument that spans the pair seems compellingly respectable: the work of a strong, modest, humorous intelligence. And yet the solution remains curiously arbitrary and personal. The argument is flawed not so much by anything in it as by the history that is around it. The choice is finally suspect *because it is a choice*. The Catholic Church is declared infallible, one must feel, not because it *is* infallible in any absolute sense, but because it is willing to *assume* that it is and Dryden is willing to *allow* that it is.

He so allows by faith, as he makes clear, and it is a faith scrupulously defined:

> God thus asserted: man is to believe
> Beyond what sense and reason can conceive.
> . . . .
> If then our faith we for our guide admit,
> Vain is the farther search of humane wit . . .
> . . . .
> Reason by sense no more can understand,
> The game is play'd into another hand.
> . . . .
> Rest then, my soul, from endless anguish freed;
> Nor sciences thy guide, nor sense thy creed.
> Faith is the best ensurer of thy bliss . . .[61]

As it stands here, this distinction is valid and necessary. The difference *must* be acknowledged. Reason and sense must not be asked to do the work of faith, and faith must not be substituted for reason and sense. Intelligence is offended by the overweening claim to "know" a great deal about God, and is equally offended by a disposition to accept on "faith" a proposition subject to proof.

And yet, left as it stands, this distinction becomes part of a series of dichotomies—faith and work, spirit and flesh, mind and body, Heaven and earth, thought and action, management and labor, poets and executives—that are ruinous in both directions. It becomes, that is, one of the sanctions of the practical divorce between quantity and quality, substance and form, work and worth, that plagues us now.

It is not necessary to assume that Dryden was *for* this sort of dualism in order to see that he rested his religious argument at a point that *allows* it. His conversion to Catholicism, as he understands it, is the result of a personal choice based on a faith that is carefully set apart from sense and reason—a choice, it seems to me, not greatly different *in kind* from the choices of the sectarian rabble that he takes so brilliantly to task in *Religio Laici*. What Dryden's struggle has revealed, beyond the terms of his final choice, is the extent to which the individual mind was by that time on its own, guided by nothing outside itself, higher than sense and reason, that had the force of truth.

We must acknowledge that in a man of Dryden's intelligence, learning, and character, his choice is a respectable and a formidable result. Its vulnerability appears when we imagine the same choice confronted by a weaker or more cynical mind as empirical truth—facts—gained ascendancy over the "superstitions" of faith. Once faith has been specialized—not only differentiated but *divided* from sense and reason—then a process has started that will finally cut the ground from under all issues of qualitative value. And so we arrive at the academic etiquette of our own day, which sets the attitude of "objective" inquiry ahead of all virtues and looks upon all qualitative judgments as "personal opinions," which it is then obliged to regard as all equal because, once the facts are settled, everybody is deemed to have a "right" to his or her "own opinion."

This process has now continued long enough, with enough results, to require some recognitions to be made: first, that belief in the sufficiency of facts or in the beneficence of technological progress is just as much a "faith" as belief in the existence or beneficence of God; and, second, that these faiths, which are assuredly not empirical, nevertheless have empirical results. Whether I believe that the Lord is my shepherd or that progress is my shepherd is a matter of practical consequence and makes a difference. The truth or value of such an "opinion" may not be provable, but it is not for that reason impotent or without effect.

I am assuming, then, that there *is* a connection joining faith to sense and reason. You cannot argue from sense and reason to faith, that is true; as Dryden said, the finite cannot grasp the infinite. But as he implies in the third part of *The Hind and the Panther*—after the main thrust of his argument is spent—you *can* and must argue from faith to reason and sense, insofar at least as consistency is to be expected between faith and conduct: a Christian should perform "Good Works" and repudiate "unrighteous Laws" and "desp'rate Cures," must work for the "*Common quiet*" that is the legitimate human concern.

In Dryden, this is left resting on the rather arbitrary ground of a personal choice beyond reason and sense. But it may be possible to draw the connection tighter. If it is possible to argue from faith to reason and sense, and if consistency is to be expected between them, then reason and sense assume a certain power to clarify and even to correct faith. That is, it is possible for an idea accepted on faith to produce worldly results that are demonstrably bad or good. If some Christians make it an article of faith that it is good to kill heathens or Communists, they will sooner or later have corpses to show for it. If some Christians believe, as alleged, that God gave them the world to do with as they please, they will sooner or later have deserts and ruins in measurable proof. If some Christians really believe that pride, lust, envy, anger, covetousness, gluttony, and sloth are deadly sins, then they will make improvements in government that will sooner or later be tangible and quantifiable.

That it is thus possible for an article of faith to be right or wrong according to worldly result suggests that we may be up against limits and necessities in our earthly experience as absolute as "the will of God" was ever taken to be, and that "the will of God" as expressed in moral law may therefore have the same standing as the laws of gravity and thermodynamics. In Dryden's day, perhaps, it was still possible to think of "love one another" as a rule contingent upon faith. By our own day such evidence has accumulated as to suggest that it may be an absolute law: Love one another or die, individually and as a species.

If so, then the difference between that law and a physical law such as the law of gravity is only a difference in the proximity of cause to effect. If I step off the roof, I will fall *immediately*; if, in this age of nuclear weapons, toxic chemicals, rampant destruction of soil, etc., we do not love one another, we or our children will suffer for it *sometime*. It is a critical difference, for it explains why people who do not ever willingly step off a roof will fearlessly regard their neighbors as enemies or competitors or economic victims. The uncertainty of the term between offense and punishment under moral law licenses all our viciousness, foolishness, and pride. Though most of us know that it is moral law—which is finally apt to look suspiciously like natural law—that visits our sins upon our children (and other people's children), still, to the worst side of our nature, deferred justice is no justice; we will rape the land and oppress the poor, and leave starvation and bloody vengeance (we hope) to be "surprises" or "acts of God" to a later generation.

Because moral justice tends not to be direct or immediate, obedience to moral law, whether or not we think it divine, becomes a matter of propriety: of asking who and where we think we are, and on whose behalf (if anyone's) we think we are acting. And it may be that these questions cannot be asked, much less answered, until the question of authority has been settled, there being, that is, no need to ask such questions if we think the only authority resides in ourselves or, as must follow, in each one of ourselves. If, on the other hand, we believe authority comes from outside or above ourselves, then those questions *must* be asked, and the answers will put us to some trouble.

The traditional view was that all authority rested in God and descended to us, on the condition of our obedience, through the ordered hierarchy of Creation. This was Milton's view, and Raphael sums it up for Adam in Book V of *Paradise Lost*:

> . . . one Almighty is, from whom
> All things proceed, and up to him return,
> If not deprav'd from good, created all
> Such to perfection, one first matter all,
> Indu'd with various forms, various degrees
> Of substance, and in things that live, of life;
> But more refin'd, more spiritous, and pure,
> As nearer to him plac't or nearer tending
> Each in thir several active Spheres assign'd,
> Till body up to spirit work, in bounds
> Proportion'd to each kind. So from the root
> Springs lighter the green stalk, from thence the leaves
> More aery, last the bright consummate flow'r
> Spirits odorous breathes: flow'rs and thir fruit
> Man's nourishment, by gradual scale sublim'd
> To vital spirits aspire, to animal,
> To intellectual, give both life and sense,
> Fancy and understanding, whence the Soul
> Reason receives, and reason is her being . . .[62]

The key to the human place in this order is in the importance and the limits given to reason. Reason comes very high; it is the "being" of souls. But it is not good in itself; Satan, after all, is an excellent reasoner. Reason is good only insofar as it serves good and is subordinate to it. As Eve says in Book IX, reason is not free to obey or disobey; it is supreme, sufficient, and free *within* obedience:

> . . . of this Tree we may not taste nor touch;
> God so commanded, and left that Command
> Sole Daughter of his voice; the rest, we live
> Law to ourselves, our Reason is our Law.[63]

This care to set bounds to reason and keep it in its place follows from recognition of its great power to do either good or evil. So far as I know, the place Milton assigns it is traditional and was understood to be its place until the nineteenth century specialized reason and imagination and turned them against each other. Pope, who is conventionally thought by those who have not read him to be the epitome of rationalism, begins *An Essay On Man* by placing the same strict limit upon reason that Milton and Dryden place upon it:

> Say first, of God above, or Man below,
> What can we reason, but from what we know?
> Of Man what see we, but his station here,
> From which to reason, or to which refer?
> Thro' worlds unnumber'd tho' the God be known,
> 'Tis ours to trace him only in our own.[64]

Reason must be so bounded because in this view of Creation *all* things must be so bounded. The order is held together by kinship, for all come both from God and from "one first matter," and this kinship is broken, the order destroyed, when one creature usurps the place of another, which of course is what happened when Adam and Eve ate the forbidden fruit. All this is restated by Dryden in *The Hind and the Panther*, in lines that understand the Fall about as Milton did, and also draw attention to the tension between Kingship and kinship, which Adam resolves by abuse of both in abuse of knowledge:

> . . . the new made man
> His Kingdom o'er his kindred world began:
> Till knowledge misapply'd, misunderstood,
> And pride of Empire sour'd his balmy bloud.
> Then, first rebelling, his own stamp he coins;
> The murth'rer *Cain* was latent in his loins . . .[65]

In all creatures, according to Milton's lines on the tree of life, the divine and the natural join. In all creatures except humans this union is untroubled. In humans it is strained because it can only be maintained by choice. What holds the two sides of our nature together is virtue, obedience to divine command. In perfect obedience, human beings would partake perfectly of both spirituality and materiality, would be both divine and natural. This seems to be true of Milton's Adam and Eve before the fall. It is true of Pope's Eden or Golden Age, in which "The state of Nature was the reign of God. . . ."[66] And it is true of Spenser's Britomart, the lady knight who represents Chastity, and who may,

like the Lady of *Comus*, be understood as a type of the unfallen
Eve. Spenser praises her as *both* "That peerelesse paterne of
Dame natures pride, / And heavenly image of perfection. . . ."[67]
As such she merits love, which Spenser understands in the Chris-
tian sense as both "deriued from aboue," and "made flesh," both
divine and natural, its two aspects united in "vertue":

> Ne henceforth be rebellious vnto loue,
> That is the Crowne of knighthood, and the band
> Of noble minds deriued from aboue,
> Which being Knit with vertue, neuer will remoue.[68]

That this "vertue," this power to unite the natural and the divine,
is the distinguishing human characteristic is suggested by the
figure of "greedie lust" in the next Canto, who "was no man,
but onely like in shape," and who desecrates his kinship with
the world: "he liu'd all on rauin and on rape / Of men and
beasts. . . ."[69]

   In *The Hind and the Panther* Dryden's understanding of faith
tends to set it apart from reason, as if the two occupied separate
spheres. But Spenser and Milton saw the two spheres as concentric, that of reason being smaller and properly subordinate to
that of faith. To this view, divine authority is both spiritual and
moral, requiring humans, if they are to *be* human, to preserve
two kinships, one with God and one with their fellow creatures
in nature. Determining what service, what work, each of these
kinships requires is the concern of decorum or propriety: considering who and where we are, *what* should we do, and *how*
should we do it? The second of these kinships is the concern, in
our time, of ecologists, and of others who wish to place their
work under the rule of ecological health. Whether the second
kinship can thrive apart from the first is a question we will probably be forced to ask.

Few poets that I know have been so explicitly appreciative of the
human kinship with the natural world as Alexander Pope, and

few have been so carefully attentive to the spiritual, moral, and practical implications of that kinship. And yet Pope has been singled out by Robert Bly in *News of the Universe* as representative of the eighteenth century's "general disdaining of nature," of the idea of "human domination of nature," of "mad optimism," of mechanical rationalism—in short, of what Mr. Bly calls "the Old Position," which he sees as opposite and inimical to the attitudes of a number of romantic, modern, oriental, and primitive poets, samples of whose work he exhibits and commends as in rebuttal. The eighteenth century was the time, he says, "when the poets were least interested in nature. It was the peak of human arrogance. Bushes were clipped to resemble carriages." The "Old Position" is summarized as "The conviction that nature is defective because it lacks reason. . . ."[70]

Pope undoubtedly has some serious shortcomings, both as a poet and as a thinker, and from the beginning he has had no lack of critics to point them out. Dr. Johnson, for instance, said of *An Essay on Man*, the only poem of Pope's quoted by Mr. Bly, "He tells us much that every man knows, and much that he does not know himself." And: "Never was penury of knowledge and vulgarity of sentiment so happily disguised."[71]

And yet it seems to me that Mr. Bly attacks this poem where it is strongest, and that it is strongest and most potentially useful to our own time where it is most traditional: in its understanding of nature and of humanity's relation to it. Though my concern with Pope goes beyond his need for defense against this attack, I wish to begin at least by speaking in his defense, for I believe that in his abuse of Pope Mr. Bly is serving an attitude or an antipathy toward Western culture that is widespread, ill-founded, and destructive.

Mr. Bly's first sample from this poem is a series of three passages (lines 189–196, 207–210, 221–232) from Epistle I:

> The bliss of man (could pride that blessing find)
> Is not to act or think beyond mankind;
> No pow'rs of body or of soul to share,

But what his nature and his state can bear.
Why has not man a microscopic eye?
For this plain reason, man is not a fly.
Say what the use, were finer optics giv'n,
T' inspect a mite, or comprehend the heav'n' . . .

Far as creations ample range extends,
The scale of sensual, mental pow'rs ascends:
Mark how it mounts, to man's imperial race,
From the green myriads in the peopled grass . . . .

How instinct varies in the grov'ling swine,
Compar'd, half-reas'ning elephant, with thine!
'Twixt that, and reason, what a nice barrier;
Forever sep'rate, yet forever near!
Remembrance and reflection how allied;
What thin partitions sense from thought divide:
And middle natures, how they long to join,
Yet never pass th' insuperable line!
Without this just gradation, could they be
Subjected, these to those, or all to thee?
The pow'rs of all subdu'd by thee alone,
Is not thy reason all these pow'rs in one?[72]

This sample contains three words, to begin with, that Mr. Bly presumably wants us to single out as particularly objectionable: "imperial," "subjected," and "subdu'd." Of "imperial" and "subjected," I will only say that they are accurate as I believe Pope understood them, and that they are severely qualified by the context, as I will show. "Subdu'd," as I assume Mr. Bly is depending on us to know, is quoted from Genesis 1:28, a text much hackneyed lately by "ecological" condemners of Western culture, who invariably construe the word as synonymous with "conquer:"

And God blessed them, and God said unto them,
Be fruitful, and multiply, and replenish the earth,
and subdue it . . .

However, the Oxford English Dictionary gives as one of the definitions of "subdue": "To bring (land) under cultivation." And in illustration of this meaning, it cites the Coverdale translation of Genesis 1:28. That this is the correct reading should be suggested immediately by its consonance with "replenish." That this is the way Pope understood it is suggested forcibly by the context.

Mr. Bly's great offense against Pope (as also and perhaps more egregiously against Milton) is in reading passages out of context—or at least in asking us to read them so. The general purpose of the sample just quoted is to show the Old Position's "lofty attitude toward nature, often expressed by imagining hierarchies inside nature with man at the top." That this falsely describes the hierarchy as Pope understands it is clear from the passage immediately following, which does not appear in Mr. Bly's book:

> Vast chain of Being, which from God began,
> Natures aethereal, human, angel, man,
> Beast, bird, fish, insect! what no eye can see,
> No glass can reach! from Infinite to thee,
> From thee to Nothing! . . .[73]

Man, then, is *not* "at the top," but somewhere in the middle of an orderly hierarchy that *joins* (it is a "chain," not a set of discrete categories) all creatures from microbes to God. That this is a chain, that it describes a necessary kinship among all the creatures that it joins, Pope understands as clearly as any ecologist:

> . . . one step broken, the great scale's destroy'd:
> From Nature's chain whatever link you strike,
> Tenth or ten thousandth, breaks the chain alike.
>   And if each system in gradation roll,
> Alike essential to th' amazing whole;
> The least confusion but in one, not all
> That system only, but the whole must fall.[74]

And he concludes the passage in the tone of a most fervent conservationist:

> All this dread ORDER break—for whom? for thee?
> Vile worm!—oh Madness, Pride, Impiety![75]

Such a hierarchy "with man at the top" would be, in current academic ecological jargon, anthropocentric. But Pope, obviously, is not an anthropocentrist; he is hardly a humanist. If man's race is "imperial," it is also subject, and this makes a great difference, for subjects do not live by their own rules—or they had better not.

In his elucidation and defense of the Chain of Being, so far as I can tell, Pope is well in line with his tradition. The old idea of universal order was earth centered, but it does not follow, as many in the "ecology movement" appear to assume, that it was man-centered. The structure of *meaning* was God-centered. One structure exactly reverses the other. This reversal is one of the events of the *Paradiso*, when Dante realizes that he is *ascending* toward the center. The earth and God, then, are *both* centers, and the axis connecting them is the Chain of Being. But as A. O. Lovejoy points out, anthropocentricity and egocentricity could not have followed from geocentricity, because, according to the old view, if the earth was the center of the universe it was also at the *bottom* of it, in the lunar sphere of change and death.

To Pope, the Chain of Being is neither mechanical nor rationalistic, but at once organic and sacred. In Epistle III, he calls it "the chain of Love:"

> See dying vegetables life sustain,
> See life dissolving vagetate again:
> All forms that perish other forms supply,
> (By turns we catch the vital breath, and die) . . .
> . . . .
> Nothing is foreign: Parts relate to whole;
> One all-extending, all-reserving Soul
> Connects each being, greatest with the least;
> Made Beast in aid of Man, and Man of Beast;
> All serv'd, all serving! nothing stands alone . . .[76]

Far from arrogant domination, humanity's proper relation to nature is that of kinship and reciprocal serving. And though this relation is full of moral and practical implications (as I will show later), humans maintain it also by love:

> Man, like the gen'rous vine, supported lives;
> The strength he gains is from th'embrace he gives.[77]

By now, we can hope to see what Pope meant when he said that "the proper study of Mankind is Man." Mr. Bly quotes this line (by itself) as evidence that Pope was not interested in nature. But the line stands, first, in defense of the proposition in the preceding line: "Know then thyself, presume not God to scan. . . ."[78] It is, then, a warning against intellectual presumption, precisely like that given by Raphael to Adam in Book VIII of *Paradise Lost*. "Man" in Pope's line obviously must mean man's estate, or the things rightfully pertaining to human life.

Mr. Bly's other sample from Pope is also taken from Epistle I (lines 99–112):

> Lo, the poor Indian! whose untutor'd mind
> Sees God in clouds, or hears him in the wind;
> His soul, proud Science never taught to stray
> Far as the solar walk, or milky way;
> Yet simple Nature to his hope has giv'n,
> Behind the cloud-topp'd hill, an humbler heav'n;
> Some safer world in depth of woods embrac'd,
> Some happier island in the wat'ry waste,
> Where slaves once more their native land behold,
> No fiends torment, no Christians thirst for gold.
> To be, contents his natural desire,
> He asks no angel's wing, no seraph's fire;
> But thinks, admitted to that equal sky,
> His faithful dog shall bear him company.[79]

Mr. Bly says that these "lines of disdain for the American Indian . . . is [*sic*] interesting in that the main evidence of inferiority that Pope mentions in the Indian is that he sees the divine in clouds and wind. To Pope that is intolerable."[80] Again, this is a tenable reading only if one ignores what immediately follows:

> Go, wiser thou! and in thy scale of sense
> Weigh thy Opinion against Providence;
> Call imperfection what thou fancy'st such,
> Say, here he gives too little, there too much;
> Destroy all creatures for thy sport or gust,
> Yet cry, If Man's unhappy, God's unjust;
> If Man alone ingross not Heav'n's high care,
> Alone made perfect here, immortal there:
> Snatch from his hand the balance and the rod,
> Re-judge his justice, be the GOD of GOD![81]

Here one needs to use some caution not to say too much in defense of Pope. So far as I know, he had never seen an Indian, and he certainly lacked our means of appreciating the complexities and qualities of American Indian cultures. To him, as to others of his time, the New World was a "romantic" place, and he once thought of writing an American pastoral in which Indians would have replaced the classical nymphs and shepherds.[82] I daresay that he would have thought of his Indian as inferior to a cultivated Englishman of the 1730s—about as he would have thought of an "untutored" Englishman.

That aside, the only evidence I can find that Pope "disdained" the Indian is that he speaks of him as "poor" and "untutored"— but both these adjectives are made at once ironical and favorable by juxtaposition with the passage that follows. The "poor Indian" is weighed against the "wiser" Englishman, much to the embarrassment of the Englishman.

No more than Mr. Bly's first sample can this passage be understood apart from Pope's traditional understanding of the Chain of Being. The point, always, is that humans are so placed in the Chain—between angels and animals, partaking of both "natures," tempted toward both—as to *endanger* it. What threatens the integrity or wholeness or health of Creation is human pride; this goes to the roots of both the Greek and the Judaic lineages of Western culture. And Pope's lines on the Indian are part of a ferocious indictment of the nature-destroying pride of his contemporaries, which, of course, led to the nature-destroying pride of

our own times. The passage concludes by making this indictment explicit:

> In Pride, in reas'ning Pride, our error lies;
> All quit their sphere, and rush into the skies.
> Pride still is aiming at the blest abodes,
> Men would be Angels, Angels would be Gods.
> Aspiring to be Gods, if Angels fell,
> Aspiring to be Angels, Men rebel . . .[83]

Here Pope's mind is concentric with the minds of great poets of
his tradition, back to the beginnings.

And so the Indian is used, in a negative sense, as an humble
club to beat the proud Englishman. It remains to ask if Pope may
not be holding up as a positive example the Indian's ability to see
divinity in nature, and I would suggest that the following lines
from the same poem indicate that Pope himself saw divinity in
nature:

> All are but parts of one stupendous whole,
> Whose body Nature is, and God the soul;
> That, chang'd thro' all, and yet in all the same,
> Great in the earth, as in th' aetherial frame,
> Warms in the sun, refreshes in the breeze,
> Glows in the stars, and blossoms in the trees,
> Lives thro' all life, extends thro' all extent,
> Spreads undivided, operates unspent,
> Breathes in our soul, informs our mortal part . . .[84]

This may be an example of the "natural religion" that Dr. Johnson and others condemned as opposed to "revelation," but in
the last line above Pope appears to be alluding to Job 34:14–15:

> . . . if he [God] gather unto himself his spirit and his breath;
> All flesh shall perish together . . .

To learn the extent to which the attitude toward nature in this
poem was rooted in Pope's own character, we may consider the
following sentences, in which Peter Quennell is quoting and par-
aphrasing from the reminiscences of Joseph Spence:

Pope's affection for the natural world—'a tree,' he declared, 'is a no-
bler object than a prince in his coronation robes'—extended to all
sentient creatures; and he distrusted the worthy Dr Hales because he
had learned that Hales practised scientific vivisection, and 'has his
hands imbrued with blood'. Did Hales, asked Spence, cut up rats?
' "Ay, and dogs too!"—(With what emphasis and concern he spoke
it.)—"Indeed, he commits most of these barbarities with the thought
of its being of use to man. But how do we know that we have a right
to kill creatures that we are so little above as dogs. . . ." ' Nor would
he agree that dogs lacked reason: 'Man has reason enough only to
know what is necessary for him to know; and dogs have just that
too. . . . They must have souls too, as imperishable in their nature as
ours. . . . Where would be the harm to us in allowing them immortal-
ity? . . . '[85]

Mr. Bly's dislike of Pope has partly to do with Pope's affirmation of hierarchy as a principle of order. And Pope did believe
that there could be no order without hierarchy; he therefore saw
it as necessary in both nature and human society:

ORDER is Heav'n's first law; and this confest,
Some are, and must be, greater than the rest,
More rich, more wise . . .[86]

The question, then, is only whether or not Pope is right. It is certainly true that human hierarchies that are inflexible or arbitrary
or oppressive are evil. The best of American and other national
histories has been made in opposition to that kind of hierarchy;
one of the best human traits is the impulse to resent and resist it.
And so a question about the worth of a given human hierarchy
involves us in a job of criticism that may take a while. But if we
ask if hierarchies exist, the answer is simply yes; they exist,
everywhere, all the time. They exist in nature as what are called
"food chains." They exist in our everyday thinking and doing;
otherwise, we would be paralyzed, would have no agenda; all
claims on our attention would be equal, and so would cancel
each other. And among all creatures there are hierarchies of ability, intelligence, and power. These discrepancies which exist by
nature, define, among humans, the need for moral law and gov-

ernmental justice. The ideal has always been a *just* hierarchy, not *no* hierarchy. A national economy, for instance, that regarded all people absolutely as equals would have the paradoxical result of making them more and more *un*equal. Wealth would be accumulated by the craftiest and the strongest—and the craftiest and the strongest, as a class, would grow steadily less numerous.

One of the most distressing things about the "ecology movement" is its ability to spawn such concepts and phrases as "ecological egalitarianism" or even "biospheric egalitarianism." These terms are distressing because they are fanciful, false alike to nature and to humanity. No such principle exists in nature. As a human principle, it either proposes suicide by starvation or it must be routinely and frequently broken. It does not tell us how to act.

Humans become, in a sense, "equal" to whatever they destroy. It appears that we are now drawing "equal" to all nature, in that sense—which means that our responsibilities have grown greater than ever before. But we cannot accept and understand our responsibilities until we acknowledge our power. Our position in the hierarchy of Creation up to ourselves—as high as Mr. Bly gives it in his summary of Pope— *is* dominant, *is* imperial, we *can* destroy everything. And it is only that dominance that defines the need for forbearance, temperance, reverence, self-control, loving-kindness, neighborliness, charity, humility, good work, husbanding, and nurturing. But the hierarchy of power is not the same as the hierarchy of value. A good human is higher than the animals on both scales; an evil human is high on the scale of power, but at the very bottom of the scale of values.

We can quarrel with the kind of human hierarchy that Pope affirmed (I dislike his prejudice in favor of great country estates), but we cannot quarrel about its existence or necessity as a principle. There are hierarchies of power, and, as Mr. Bly obviously believes, there are hierarchies of value. What needs to be understood, from Pope as from the ecologists, is that what is inferior in power or value may nevertheless be indispensable. To a starving man or fox, a rabbit is inferior but indispensable. A horse is more valuable than a horseshoe, but in certain circumstances the horseshoe is indispensable. I have seen a "biospheric egalitarian" condemnation of Christianity because it holds that humans are more valuable than sparrows, but the Christian point is the one that I have been making: sparrows are indispensable; God loves them, and knows of the fall of each one. (I do not expect to run into any "biospheric egalitarian" who would need to flip a coin to choose between a child and a sparrow.)

The indispensability of things small or unknown is the principle that most strongly argues for the extension of the Chain of Being above the level of humans. We are obviously subject to something we do not understand—why else would we be making so many mistakes? What the old believers in the Chain of Being have to say to us is that if we conceive ourselves as the subjects of God, whose law is in part the law of nature, then there is some hope that we can right ourselves and behave with decency within the community of creatures. We will be spared the clumsiness, waste, and grave danger of trying to make up our own rules.

In the lines counterpoised against the description of "the poor Indian" ("Go, wiser thou! and in thy scale of sense / Weigh thy opinion against Providence . . ."), Pope is voicing an old fear of mechanical manipulation. This fear is surely manifested in the ancient prohibitions against greed and lust, which reduce creatures to quantities and "things." And perhaps we have as part of our definition a certain horror of mechanical interference with natural law. There has at least always been a number of us who have had a strong, deep aversion to proposals to move the earth by leverage or to transmute some "base" thing into gold. This is rooted, I think, in the suspicion, the faith, that there is more to reality than is apparent to such manipulators.

Spenser makes a parable of this in *The Faerie Queene* (V, II, xxx–liv); it seems plausible that Pope took his "scale of sense" from this very passage. Sir Artegall, the knight representing Justice, and Talus, his iron page, having come "nigh to the sea,"

> beheld a mighty Gyant stand
> Vpon a rocke, and holding forth on hie
> An huge great paire of ballance in his hand,
> With which he boasted in his surquedrie,
> That all the world he would weigh equallie,
> If ought he had the same to counterpoys.[87]

It is the Gyant's notion that the four elements have got out of balance and therefore need to be weighed and portioned out equally again. He is surrounded by a crowd of "the vulgar" who

> cluster thicke vnto his leasings vaine,
> Like foolish flies about an hony crocke,
> In hope by him great benefite to gaine,
> And vncontrolled freedome to obtaine.[88]

Artegall first suggests that some caution is in order:

> All change is perillous, and all chaunce vnsound.
> Therefore leaue off to weigh them all againe,
> Till we may be assur'd they shall their course retaine.[89]

Whereupon the Gyant calls him a "foolishe Elfe" and makes an argument that shows him to be a most idealistic and thorough egalitarian:

> Seest not, how badly all things present bee . . .
> . . . .
> Were it not good that wrong were then surceast,
> And from the most, that some were giuen to the least?
>
> Therefore I will throw downe these mountaines hie,
>   And make them leuell with the lowly plaine:
>   These towring rocks, which reach vnto the skie,
>   I will thrust downe into the deepest maine,
>   And as they were, them equalize againe.
>   Tyrants that make men subiect to their law,
>   I will suppresse, that they no more may raine;
>   And Lordings curbe, that commons ouer-aw;
> And all the wealth of rich men to the poore will draw.[90]

Artegall then asks, appropriately I think:

> Of things vnseene how canst thou deeme aright,

....

> Sith thou misdeem'st so much of things in sight?[91]

And he goes on to develop an idea exactly opposite to the Gyant's:

> All creatures must obey the voice of the most hie.

> They liue, they die, like as he doth ordaine,
>   Ne eurer any asketh reason why.
>   The hils doe not the lowly dales disdaine;
>   The dales doe not the lofty hils enuy.
>   He maketh Kings to sit in souerainty;
>   He maketh subjects to their powre obay . . .[92]

As a political argument, this offers a sorry pair of choices; it involves a dangerous confusion between human order and natural order. The human economy, insofar as it uses nature, must be made in respect for, and in analogy with, the processes by which nature preserves and renews itself. But a human society must preserve these processes by moral laws, which are *not* natural. Spenser's defense of monarchy as "natural" is no different from later defenses of the "naturalness" of plutocracy. However, if we read it only as an argument about natural order, we take Artegall's side, and we see Spenser's point: it is dangerous to meddle with "things unseen," especially if one mistakes or misjudges "things in sight"; and anyone willing to meddle in this way is a monster—a "Gyant."

As one reads through this episode, one's feelings about it grow more and more complicated; Artegall is a poor hero to a democrat, and his justice is "frontier justice"; the justice of his iron page, a sort of comic book avenger, is even rougher. And yet, to a twentieth-century reader, the feeling of *déjà vu* is undeniable. At the beginning, anyhow, it is hard not to feel that one is reading an allegory of our own time. What the Gyant is proposing is a "scientific breakthrough" that will right all wrong. And he is supported by a crowd hoping for easy wealth and "vncontrolled freedom." There is not the least taint of modesty or humility in this Gyant. He is an early devotee of the Big Thought; though he boasts of the minute exactitude of his scales, "he of little things made reckoning light. . . ."[93]

Whatever one thinks of Artegall and his justice, Spenser's understanding of the meaning of uncontrolled freedom is correct: it means tyranny by the most powerful. And he is correct too in his assumption that one function of justice is to limit freedom in the use of power. If the strong are permitted to use *all* their power, then the less strong have no power at all. This is the point of the first episode of the same Canto, in which Artegall kills a "cursed cruel Sarazin," who has been robbing and murdering travelers at a bridge, and leaves the Sarazin's head upon a pole

> To be a mirrour to all mighty men,
> In whose right hands great power is contayned,
> That none of them the feeble ouerren,
> But alwaies doe their powre within iust compasse pen.[94]

This idea of just compass can be derived only from such an idea as the Chain of Being, for without the idea of hierarchical order the just compass of any human must be defined solely by power—power, that is, *replaces* justice.

Read critically, as any poet should be read, Spenser is a good teacher of morals, a good teacher *about* morals. C. S. Lewis speaks of *The Faerie Queene* as "health-giving," and I agree that it is. But Spenser is not much help when it comes to practical, everyday application of his principles. His exemplary people are all living in Faerie Land and most of them do not have regular jobs. *The Faerie Queene* is short on domestic economy.

English poetry strikes me as short on domestic economy. Jonson, in "To Penshurst" and "To Sir Robert Wroth," gives us a careful understanding of hospitality, stewardship, and charity as practiced by the best country nobility. But his point of view is that of a grateful guest, and in spite of his praise of "high huswifery," he has nothing very practical to say. Marvell's *Upon Appleton House*, a profound meditation on agrarian life, with its exemplary movement from house to field to woods, is the work of a brilliant observer, describer, and interpreter of a place both human and natural, but though we see something of the work of the place, we learn little of the husbandry and wifery of it. This is not meant as a critical statement about those particular poems, but it may be a critical *fact* that up to Pope no appreciable English poet gave us anything resembling the *Georgics* or *Works and Days*. That is, though they give us often enough the look and feel of country life—and sometimes, as in Shakespeare, the sound of it too—they give us no grasp of how it works or ought to work. They tell us how love, war, politics, and social life work and ought to work, but they do not tell us how all this fitted or ought to have fitted into nature. They do not offer us much that can *directly* inform or clarify or instruct us in the *use* of nature.

That they did not is understandable; there were, after all, hereditary classes and work lineages that could be trusted to preserve the skills and the practical lore of husbandry and wifery. But that the poets took little or no interest in these "low" disciplines and economies may indicate that such things were thought unworthy of the attention of the best minds. And *that* can indicate a serious weakness. "High culture" can be too "high," can separate itself too far from low culture—the result being that the people most empowered to act in relation to nature no longer know *how* to act. I do not mean to suggest that such concerns are incumbent upon any particular poet; but if a *culture* goes for too long without producing poets and others who concern themselves with the problems and proprieties of humanity's practical connection to nature, then the work of all poets may suffer, and so may nature.

Pope is remarkable, among other reasons, for having addressed himself to these problems fairly directly. I say *fairly* directly because he was not a farmer and was not attracted to the farmstead arts. But he *was* a countryman (Mr. Bly speaks of his "visits to the country," forgetting that, as a Catholic, Pope was forbidden to live within ten miles of London; his "visits" were to the city), and he was a gardener. Not only was the garden on his little place at Twickenham "an accomplished work of art," but Pope, with Lord Burlington and Burlington's gardener, William Kent, was deeply involved in a movement to reform English gardening. Mr. Bly is also wrong to suppose that topiary shrubbery was typical of English gardening in the eighteenth century. Such geometrical formality was "old-fashioned" by 1712, when Pope ridiculed it in "an ambitious disquisition on the modern art of gardening." The influence of Chinese gardening had been felt, and the new ideal was harmony between the garden and the surrounding countryside and between the natural and the artificial. Peter Quennell says that, as a gardener, Lord Burlington aspired to the effect of "a delicate equipoise between Man and the surrounding universe."⁹⁵

Such principles may be seen as implicit in *An Essay on Man*, but Pope makes them explicit in the *Epistle to Burlington*, a poem about gardening, or what we would now call "landscaping." All gardening, of course, *uses* nature, and so the gardener always works in the presence of the possibility of *mis*use. Humans are understood correctly as nature-using and nature-changing creatures. Even the unfallen Adam and Eve in *Paradise Lost* did "rural work"; they pruned the fruit trees, and "led the Vine / To wed her Elm."⁹⁶ They used and changed nature. This is true of all peoples, and in varying degrees of all wild creatures. The question is not one of ecological egalitarianism or pacifism, but of harmony between part and whole. Pope's ideal was to use nature—like all gardeners, he meant to "improve" her—without disharmony. His rule was: "In all, let Nature never be forgot." And he said: "Consult the Genius of the Place in all. . . ."⁹⁷ Raymond Williams writes that this "Genius of the Place" is merely "an invitation to arrange and rearrange nature according to a point of view. . . ."⁹⁸ But that suggests that Pope is using the phrase merely as fancy talk; the phrase may have some irony in it, but I don't think Pope is being frivolous. The genius of a place is its guardian spirit; Pope knew that, and he knew, as is clear from his exposition of the Chain of Being, that abuse of "things in sight" abuses "things unseen." Human work done in a place should not affront its "Genius"—and we may read "Genius" either as guardian spirit or as the mostly invisible order or whole to which the place belongs, or both. But even more than that is meant: if the "Genius of the Place" is not offended, it will help; it "Paints as you plant, and as you work, designs."[99] Gardening is neither wholly natural, nor wholly artificial, but both; it is a collaboration between the gardener and nature. Pope, I think, is alluding to the principle, commonly understood by good farmers and gardeners, that nature *responds* to good treatment. The gardener must never forget nature because nature, as much as human intention, indicates what must be done—that is, "designs."

In this poem Pope puts a considerable emphasis on use: " 'Tis Use alone that sanctifies Expense. . . ." But this does not mean that he thought everything in nature should be used. He emphasized use because use is the key to a just correspondence between acts and needs, and because he hated ostentation, extravagance, waste, useless show. The ideal, as we see perhaps more plainly in the *Epistle to Bathurst*, is hospitality, charity domiciled: "With Splendor, Charity; with Plenty, Health . . ." for "Wealth in the gross is death. . . ."[100]

These two *Epistles* have an obvious kinship to the opening stanzas of *Upon Appleton House*, in which Marvell speaks his dislike of "Man unrul'd" and "unproportioned dwellings" and praises Appleton House because "all things are composed here / Like Nature, orderly and near . . ." and "ev'ry Thing does answer Use." Humans, like birds, burrowing animals, and tortoises, should have dwellings proportioned to their size: "Their Bodies measure out their Place."[101]

That Marvell and Pope thought the bodies of Lords and Ladies a good deal larger than we think them is a matter that ought not to obscure for us the working of a kind of formal intelligence that is both beautiful and practical, and that is evident in the work of other poets in this tradition, though it seems to me nowhere so painstakingly developed as in Pope. The proper question for us is not who was practicing the principles, but whether or not the principles are good. Would things now be better or worse if since Pope's time we had "let Nature never be forgot," and if before changing or building on any place we had consulted its "Genius"? They would, of course, be a great deal better.

It is a mistake to look in Pope for "pure" nature, but then it is probably a mistake to look for "pure" nature in the work of his predecessors. To Pope and the other believers in the Chain of Being, nature included *all* bodied creatures. Pope's nature has humans in it; his humans have nature in them. In Pope there is no wish "to turn and live with animals," for he assumes that we *do* live with them as fellow creatures. The question, for him, is whether we shall live with them as fellow animals, in which case we will brutalize them and ourselves, or as humans, in which case we will recognize their right to their necessary place in the order of things.

Nor in Pope does the wild gander cry "*Ya-honk*" as it does so suddenly and finely in the midst of *Song of Myself*. Unhuman nature does not appear in his pages in its own estate and right as it does in Gary Snyder's. But that would be regrettable only if we had no pages but Pope's in which to look for it. The remarkable thing is that though their ways of considering nature differ significantly, Pope and Mr. Snyder ask the same practical questions about it: How do we fit in? What is the possibility of a human harmony *within* nature?

To Pope, nature included us and all our material works and was orderly; therefore the making of *any* human artifact—a garden, a house, a poem—raised inescapable practical questions about where it belonged, what its size should be, how it should be made, how it would fit its surroundings. These are all questions of propriety, and between Pope and Gary Snyder I think that they were not much asked. Most poets have not asked them, nor, except for the ecologists, have most scientists; the industrialists and technologists certainly have not. The working assumption has been that we are *not* part of, or dependent on, an order superior to ourselves. And the logical extension of that is not a benign humanist commonwealth—"liberty, equality, and fraternity"—but the so-called "jungle law," every man for himself, every poem for itself, the law of industry and the modern age.

This law and all its corollaries, erected upon a subsidy of squandered soil and "cheap" fossil fuel, falsified the world and made it a limited thing of human fantasy. But once we see and say, with Mr. Snyder, that we are "hemmed in by mysteries / all moving in order,"[102] that false world of abstract, inflatable quantities falls away; we then see clearly the forms and motions of visible things and events, [103] and so are prepared for "the real work": "to make the world as real as it is, and to find ourselves as real as we are within it."[104] The real work, if I understand Mr. Snyder correctly, consists of the local jobs of right livelihood, right neighborhood, and caretaking. I don't think that Mr. Snyder went back to Pope for this, but the same movement of the spirit, the same clearing of the eyes, is in Pope. Having acknowledged the invisible order that harmonizes Creation and allows humanity its proper and becoming place, Pope saw:

> Not man alone, but all that roam the wood,
> Or wing the sky, or roll along the flood,
> Each loves itself, but not itself alone . . .[105]

It is an order of love, but love is not enough; love must act, find its work, do it well. The invisible order proposes a visible order. The order of nature proposes a human order in harmony with it. These are beautiful ideas, but their beauty cannot be separated from their practicality. The principles that Pope sets out in *The Epistle to Burlington* are meant immediately to govern the improvement of a country estate, but they would serve as well for the making of a farm, a town, a factory, a highway, a sanitation system. They are esthetically sound; they are also sound ecologically; they are eminently practical—and we will find, I believe, that they have each of these qualities because they have the others.

Exactly Pope's kind of concern for propriety in the human use of nature reappears in England two centuries later in the work of the great agricultural scientist, Sir Albert Howard. Howard founded his work on the perception that a healthy agriculture could not be oriented to any human economy, but had to be oriented to nature, to "the Wheel of Life," as he called it. One cannot act well or beneficently in a place until one has understood its *nature*, precedent to human intention. Thus, in country originally forested, the farmer must study the forest, because, to be healthy, the field must be an analogue of the forest; in analogy its nature is remembered. The nature of the original forest is, so to speak, "the Genius of the Place," which one is obliged to consult, not by human prescription, but by natural law. It is perhaps not without significance that in describing "Nature's farming," Howard reverts to allegory:

> The main characteristic of Nature's farming can therefore be summed up in a few words. Mother earth never attempts to farm without live stock; she always raises mixed crops; great pains are taken to preserve the soil and to prevent erosion; the mixed vegetable and animal wastes are converted into humus; there is no waste; the processes of growth and the processes of decay balance one another; ample provision is made to maintain large reserves of fertility; the greatest care is taken to store the rainfall; both plants and animals are left to protect themselves against disease.[106]

The same sort of thinking appears again in the present time in the work of the Kansas agricultural critic and plant geneticist Wes Jackson, who argues that the severe problems of Midwestern grain fields are explained by their differences from the prairie ecosystems that preceded them. And he argues, like Howard, that these problems can be solved by making a new kind of grain field which would be analogous to the diversified perennial plant communities of the natural prairie. If the necessary associations of perennial grain-bearing plants can be developed, then soil erosion will cease to be a problem, losses to pests and diseases will be insignificant, and production costs will be greatly reduced.[107]

But nowhere, so far as I know, has this kind of thought been more particularly worked out than in the "bioshelters" designed and built by John Todd and his associates at the New Alchemy Institute. Mr. Todd started from the perception that the conventional or orthodox suburban house "represents a failure of design." Though it more than adequately shelters its human occupants, the conventionally designed house incorporates the pattern of industrial consumption: its relation to the world outside itself is parasitic; it consumes finite resources, and produces "wastes" that clutter and pollute the surroundings; it opposes technology to biology. The principles, the industrial assumptions, of its design make it ultimately self-destructive.

To escape the inherent violence of those principles, Mr. Todd undertook to design a house that would harmonize or rhyme with and within a series of analogous structures in nature:

> There is a unity of structure extending from the gene to the planet. The genius of nature lies in its ability to fuse the opposites of autonomy and interdependence to create a whole.

It is precisely this harmony and interdependence of natural forms that industrial thought first ignores and then destroys by *acting* on the assumption that the whole is not an order but only a *sum* of discrete and therefore expendable items or quantities. The conventional modern house is one of the enactments of this assumption, protecting one couple or family at the expense of virtually everything else.

But the human principle implicit in the natural series of structures is that whatever contains is contained, and obligation and responsibility must therefore move in *two* directions, both inward and outward. The house must not only protect its human residents; it must protect as well its—and their—place in nature. It was therefore necessary to design not just a house, a "residence," but a household, a place where a family's inward and outward needs and responsibilities could achieve an orderly meeting.

The bioshelter idea, then, proposes to make a household on the pattern of an ecosystem, adapted to the local landscape and climate, using local materials. The house itself is "empowered by the same forces that govern the biosphere. . . ." Its energy comes from sun and wind. It aims to be human in scale, rejecting the "gigantism" that has proved so fatal because so unadaptive a trait. It balances consumption with production so far as possible, incorporating greenhouses, fish tanks, a tree nursery, etc. Wherever possible, it substitutes biology for physics, living things for mechanical devices. Its governing principle is symbiosis: the food production system heats the house; the fish tanks raise fish, heat the greenhouse, provide irrigation water and fertilizer for the plants.[108]

It is important to see that Mr. Todd's basic design principles, which are inherently and complexly practical, are also esthetic, for they have to do with the ancient artistic proprieties of place and scale; they propose the same careful remembrance of nature that Pope thought essential to poet and gardener alike; and their aim is balance, coherence, and harmony. The bioshelters spring from an understanding of biology and ecology, not from any great tradition of building, and yet John Todd's principles have a certain kinship with the best kind of traditional architecture. The English critic and cultural historian, H. J. Massingham, has written perceptively of the harmony between a building and its place expressed by local traditions of workmanship, now lost: "the infallible and unconscious act of adjusting buildings to the ground on which they stood. . . ." He speaks of "the modern house in its crude heresy against the natural law of fitness to environment." And then of the traditional buildings "that do express an organic relation with their surroundings," he says:

> The cottages, barns and farmsteads seem to sink into this patient relaxed earth, as though her cloak were thrown over them. They are subdued to earth as earth is to sky. Subdued too in the sense of ac-

cepting their limitations by the building of them in the local materials.[109]

Massingham's point of view is esthetic, but in implication practical, the opposite of Mr. Todd's, but the principles and the feeling for what is proper seem much the same. The point, I think, is
that if the principles are right, there is no incompatibility between the esthetic and the practical; each is implicit in the other.

It would seem to follow that, if the principles are right, there is
no inherent or necessary incompatibility between art and science, or even between art and applied science. The aim of both
would be harmonious collaboration between human and natural genius, which, as Pope saw, must always involve the acceptance of nature as co-designer. It may be that disharmony between human disciplines (and mental functions) necessarily
results in disharmony between disciplines (and minds) and nature.

It would be folly, of course, to suppose that Alexander Pope,
Gary Snyder, Sir Albert Howard, Wes Jackson, John Todd, and
many generations of rural English builders all belong to the same
"school" or pattern of influence. But I think that there would be
no folly in supposing that they all are allied to something peren-
nially and changelessly true of the connection between nature
and human nature; and I think that this truth may be close to
what Pope calls "sense." In gardening, he says, good sense is
"more needful than Expence, / And . . . previous ev'n to
Taste. . . ." It is Heaven's gift, "A Light, which in yourself you
must perceive. . . ."[110] Sense is the soul of art, for it governs the
relations of parts to one another and to the whole. It is the understanding of what a part is, and how it should behave, as a part.
This is the human power to which the Genius of the Place responds, and with which it collaborates; if you follow sense in
your work, you will have powerful allies: "Nature shall join you;
Time shall make it grow / A Work to wonder at. . . ."[111] The hu-
mor of Pope's satires rests upon such sense—if we do not know
what good sense is, we do not know what absurdity is or what it

means—and it becomes the measure of experience in the novels of Jane Austen. It is the old decorum or propriety, the intelligence of what is fitting or seemly or becoming in the parts of a garden or a poem or in the behavior of a human being. If one knows where one is in the hierarchical, the vertical, order, then one can *see* where one is in the horizontal order, in the world, and one can attain seemly competences of whereabouts.

In the fifth Canto of *The Rape of the Lock* Pope writes:

> How vain are all these glories, all our pains,
> Unless good sense preserve what beauty gains . . .
> . . . .
> Oh! if to dance all night, and dress all day,
> Charm'd the small-pox, or chas'd old-age away;
> Who would not scorn what huswife's cares produce,
> Or who would learn one earthly thing of use?[112]

If one knows both poems, it is hard not to set these lines beside the last lines of the "Ode on a Grecian Urn." Sensibility triumphs over sense in Keats's poem, and it is finally less satisfactory. Keats says that "Beauty is truth . . . "—meaning artistic beauty and, by implication, the beauty of idealized nature, youth, and love. But Pope's attention is on the temporal, mortal world as "the right place for love," and therefore he insists also upon the beauty of "good sense." *The Rape of the Lock* is a poem against egotistical passion, and in that respect it belongs to a grand family of works extending from *The Iliad* and the Bible to *Sense and Sensibility*. Pope's life's work can be usefully read, I suspect, as a long study of the silliness, wastefulness, violence, and *dullness* of egotistical passion.

"Things reveal themselves passing away," Yeats said. The idea of the Chain of Being seems to lie under English poetry like a root, sending up sprouts, nourishing and informing an essential sanity. In the work of Pope its whole energy bursts out into the light, flowers, and disappears. The Chain idea perhaps lingered on in the form of a ladder, biological or social, up which creatures evolved or climbed. And then the ladder was laid down and became a railroad or highway along which we "progress" toward "new horizons" where we will all be free, equal, educated—and rich. That is too neat a scheme, for human hierarchies of money and power still remain, but there is some truth in it; the old sense of hierarchy that defined our power in terms of responsibility has been lost. The comely and becoming belief in the orderliness of creation has been fretted away by the contentions of egotistical passion and its inevitable result, egotistical despair. The individual has moved, so to speak, between himself and the world.

Less than a hundred years after the *Epistle to Burlington* and *An Essay on Man*, William Hazlitt was writing about the egotism of the "modern" poets. Of Wordsworth, he said: "He chooses to have his subject a foil to his invention, to owe nothing but to himself."[113] To "a modern school of poetry" (evidently the lake poets) he attributed the "great fault"

> that it is an experiment to reduce poetry to a mere effusion of natural sensibility; or, what is worse, to divest it both of imaginary splendour and human passion, to surround the meanest objects with the morbid feelings and devouring egotism of the writers' own minds . . . their minds reject, with a convulsive effort and intolerable loathing, the very idea that there ever was, or was thought to be, anything superior to themselves.[114]

And he says of this school again:

> According to the prevailing notions, all was to be natural and new. Nothing that was established was to be tolerated. . . . Everyone did that which was good in his own eyes.[115]

It was possible to explain this: "Our poetical literature had, towards the close of the last century, degenerated into the most trite, insipid, and mechanical of all things. . . ."[116] But Hazlitt knew that the reaction was disproportionate. We are now in a better position than Hazlitt to see how extreme it was, for it has become more extreme. It was part of a disintegration that has not stopped.

I have no detailed knowledge of the steps of the transformation from the traditional ideas of order and propriety still alive in Pope to the modern egotism. My interest is merely to understand the difference, and for this purpose the case of Shelley may be of crucial importance. No one better fits Hazlitt's definition of poetic egotism than Shelley, and he did nothing more characteristic of himself than to participate in the romantic misunderstanding of Satan as the hero and superior moral being of *Paradise Lost*.

This misunderstanding can be *partly* attributed to the fault of *Paradise Lost* that I discussed earlier. One of the consequences of Milton's decision to make God a visible figure or character in his poem is that he made Him a tyrant—as any omnipotent *character* must be. There is a great difference between attributing omnipotence or unalterable law to a mysterious Creator and attributing it to a personified deity on a throne. As Dante apparently understood, human imagination is not copious or comprehensive enough to unite omnipotence with infinite justice, mercy, and love in the same character. But what Shelley failed to see is that though Satan is *represented* to some extent as a political rebel against an omnipotent person, his behavior is *understood* in the scriptural sense as prideful and inordinate. What he holds in contempt is not God's person (which he envies) or God's power (which he desires), but God's law and the embodiment of that law in the Creation. It is of this aspect of God as orderly workman, maker of Heaven and earth, that Raphael is spokesman, and I would maintain that he is the superior moral presence in the poem.

To make Satan the hero and to think him in any simple sense magnificent is surely to dismiss the historical and biographical difficulty of *Paradise Lost* and to make it much less useful and instructive than it is. But it also flings away the poem's traditional idea of order with one hand, and, with the other, makes nothing of Milton's struggle with the problems of authority and obedience. If Satan is the hero, then authority is given entirely to

the consciences and desires of individuals, and rebellion becomes—as Dryden apparently feared—an absolute imperative.
That is, Shelley's identification of (and with) Satan as a hero generalizes the principle of rebellion beyond any issue. The principle becomes absolute, and it absolutely repudiates the principles
of hierarchy and subordination. It becomes a kind of ultimate
protestantism. *Any* authority or superiority is seen as an occasion to rebel and overthrow.

There is an odd sympathy in Shelley for Lady Macbeth that
may be symptomatic of this. In *A Defense of Poetry*, he quotes
directly from her speech to Macbeth (I. vii. 39–45): "But we let
'*I dare not* wait upon *I would*, like the poor cat in the adage.' "[117]
It might be argued that the context makes this innocuous
enough; the saying is apt here; he is talking about the will to use
the "moral, political and historical wisdom" that we now have
to bring "scientific and economical knowledge" under the rule
of justice. But, whether consciously or not, he paraphrases a
more significant part of the same speech in "Julian and Mad-
dalo:"

> we might be all
> We dream of, happy, high, majestical.
> Where is the love, beauty and truth we seek
> But in our mind? and if we were not weak
> Should we be less in deed than in desire?[118]

The speaker of these lines is Julian, who speaks for Shelley. And
the speech is full of a mischief that can be appropriately described as Satanic. What support has the notion that "we might
be all / We dream of, happy, high, majestical"? All available evidence is against it. Traditional wisdom says that we cannot—indeed, *should* not—be all we dream of. But Shelley, like Milton's
Satan, immediately wrests his desire out of the external circumstance that would disprove and invalidate it and makes off with
it into his mind: "Where is the love, beauty and truth we seek /
But in our mind?" And here, just before he remembers Lady

Macbeth, he remembers Milton's Satan, whose most blasphemous lines are quoted approvingly in *A Defense of Poetry*:

> The mind is its own place, and of itself
> Can make a Heaven of Hell, a Hell of Heaven.[119]

These lines are quoted in support of the assertion that "All things
exist as they are perceived: at least in relation to the percipient."
And they are followed by what Shelley apparently meant as an
elaboration: *poetry* is the power of the mind that enables it to
escape the authority of a tyrannical God: "But poetry defeats the
curse which binds us to be subjected to the accident of surrounding impressions."[120] I am unsure how to read "surrounding
impressions," for impressions are not usually thought capable
of surrounding anything, but from the context I assume he
means external circumstance or physical whereabouts. If, then,
the mind is elected as a "place," one's place in the world becomes
an "accident."

Events, I think, comment sufficiently upon these lines. The
great economic discovery of modern times is that vast numbers
of people can be made to believe that "we might be all / We dream
of . . . ," and that, though there may be no correspondence
whatever between this belief and any history or hope, people so
believing will *buy* things. And we are now surrounded by the
most insistent evidence that a mind that elects itself a place maintains itself as such by the ruin of earthly places. One cannot divide one's mind from its earthly place, preferring the inner place
to the outer, without denying the mind's care to the earthly
place.

I certainly do not think that Shelley advocated such results.
But there can be no doubt that he advocated the division that has
caused them. Shelley's case is not a simple one. He is both preem-
inently gifted and severely flawed. So much brilliance so much
involved in the complications and bewilderments that still afflict
us is bound to be instructive to us and is bound to baffle us. My
problem with *A Defense of Poetry* is that I mainly agree with his

understanding of the importance and the usefulness of imagination, but could not more strongly disagree with his insistence upon dividing imagination from reason, giving poetry entirely to imagination; and where I disagree I cannot be certain to what extent he consciously intends to go as far as he does in this division and to approve its implications, or to what extent he is unconsciously carried along by the momentum of his principle of rebellion.

At any rate, his divorce of the spiritual from the physical and of poetry from the material world is absolute:

> A poet participates in the eternal, the infinite, and the one; as far as relates to his conceptions, time and place and number are not.[121]

And language also is made unearthly, divested of its power of reference to material things: it "is arbitrarily produced by the imagination, and has reference to thoughts alone. . . ."[122] But though he so fiercely dissociates imagination from reason, he yet wants reason, in the works of "mechanists" and "political economists," to be ruled by "those first principles which belong to the imagination. . . ."[123] Poetry, as he puts it later, should control selfishness, for "Poetry, and the principle of Self, of which money is the visible incarnation, are the God and Mammon of the world."[124]

Of course, this does not work. Once imagination is divided from reason and from the material world, it loses its power over them; it loses, or begins to lose, even its power to refer to them. Shelley was right in seeing that reason, economics, and mechanical technology needed to be controlled by some higher power or law. But he was wrong to suppose that imagination, so insistently defined as "superior" and so strictly set apart, could exert any such control. He was wrong, even, in supposing that imagination, so defined, could remain superior to "the principle of Self." When this sort of division takes place, as Hazlitt saw, *everything* is made to serve that principle. *All* pure and separate things are in some sense out of control. Spirituality and materiality, body and soul, need each other, live in each other; divided, they come to nothing. Or they become destructive of each other.

But Shelley's governing principle is division, always empowered by the impulse of personal rebellion. In rebellion against the demands and difficulties of earthly and bodily life, he goes off into the world of spirit or mind. He would have us believe that this is a "higher" world, an ideal realm—and sometimes it may be. But Shelley is unsure of the difference between the ideal realm of Platonic perfection and the realm of his own desiring and willing mind, and so he does not always know whether he is in Paradise or only in Dreamland, whether he is involved in a triumph of imagination or an "escape from reality."

All this is painfully clear in *Epipsychidion*, surely one of the most exalted raptures ever lifted upon the wings of sexual fantasy.

The poem is "Addressed to the Noble and Unfortunate Lady Emilia V——, Now Imprisoned in the Convent of ——," with whom Shelley, equally unfortunate, is in love. This is a doomed love, partly because it is too high and fine for this world, partly because the lovers were not born "twins of the same mother," partly because Shelley's wife will not accept the young lady as a "sister." The poem's first 150 lines consist mainly of a rout of epithets that collide and ricochet like a load of birdshot in an iron kettle. Emily is addressed as a "Sweet Spirit," a "Poor captive bird," a "High, spirit-winged Heart," a "Seraph of Heaven," a "Sweet Benediction"; as a "Glory," a "Moon," a "living Form Among the Dead," a "Star," a "Wonder," a "Beauty," a "Terror," a "Harmony of Nature's art," a "Mirror"; as a "Sweet Lamp," "A lovely soul," "A well of sealed and secret happiness," "A Star" (again), "A smile," "a gentle tone," "A beloved light," "A Solitude, a Refuge, a Delight"; as "A lute," "a buried treasure," "A cradle of young thoughts of wingless pleasure; / A violet-shrouded grave of Woe"; as "a mortal shape indued / With love and life and light and deity," "An image of some bright Eternity; / A shadow of some golden dream; a Splendour," "A tender Reflection of the eternal Moon of Love," "A Metaphor of Spring and Youth and Morning; / A Vision like incarnate April"; as "Spouse! Sister! / Angel! Pilot of the Fate / Whose course has been so starless!" There can be no doubt, after all this, that the poet is full of powerful feelings, but what the nature or quality of his feeling may be becomes less clear with every additional epithet. One cannot define or designate anything precisely by calling it, in passing, thirty-eight different things. The critical point to be made here is that after so much effort, we do not know dependably a single thing about the history, the appearance, or the character of the unfortunate Emilia that we had not learned already from the subtitle.

This declaration of love is followed by an attack on marriage, which, under the circumstances, a man burning with such an exalted flame cannot be expected to admire. He calls it

> that great sect
> Whose doctrine is, that each one should select
> Out of the crowd a mistress or a friend,
> And all the rest, though fair and wise, commend
> To cold oblivion . . .[125]

Thus defined, of course, marriage is easily condemned. But only blind determination could put this construction upon marital fidelity. If he is talking about Christian marriage, then neighborly love and charity would forbid commending others "to cold oblivion." That is not at all what is meant by "forsaking all others," as Shelley must have known. Anyhow, he does not approve of marriage, which is not comprehensive enough for him, and he speaks of it also as slavery and as "the dreariest and the longest journey."[126]

There follows a passage on the nature of "True Love," which in another version he calls "Free Love":

> True Love in this differs from gold and clay,
> That to divide is not to take away.[127]

Shelley is said to have taken this idea from *Purgatorio* XV, where it is love of the Good that is increased "by partnership." Love of the Good undoubtedly does increase the more it is shared or divided. Familial and neighborly love increases by division the same way—though here there may be a limit. But Shelley is writing about what is properly called "a consuming passion" and the growth of that sort of love by division seems extremely doubtful. If practiced as recommended, the result would be a spectacular increase in the population of orphanages and graveyards. It does no good, I think, to call this a Platonic poem or to say that it idealizes Emilia. Shelley wanted badly to make this a "spiritual" poem; he called it "a mystery; as to real flesh and blood, you know I do not deal in these articles."[128] But he was able to carry it only so far as fantasy.

The reason it does not become spiritual as, say, Spenser's *Epithalamion* does, is that Shelley is so unwilling for it to be anything else. He does not really intend to "divide" love; after the passing reference to Mrs. Shelley, this poem is inhabited solely by himself and Emilia, or by the phantom so named. What he is intent upon dividing are kinds of experience and functions of mind, beginning with his fundamental and characteristic differentiation of "mind" from "its object":

> Mind from its object differs most in this:
> Evil from good; misery from happiness;
> The baser from the nobler; the impure
> And frail, from what is clear and must endure.[129]

There is virtually no syntax here, but the gist is fairly plain: Shelley is on mind's side, and mind has scored *all* the points. Furthermore:

> If you divide suffering and dross, you may
> Diminish till it is consumed away;
> If you divide pleasure and love and thought,
> Each part exceeds the whole . . .[130]

I am not sure that I understand the first two lines, but it seems unlikely that you can diminish suffering or dross by division. The next statement defies comprehension; it not only misuses Dante, but turns him upside down. What we have here is a new law made to order for the fallen Angels. For anyone who wishes to be "free," here is the text; if the divided part exceeds the whole, then the whole has no standing and its existence implies no restraint. But, of course, parts in this condition cannot be *located* in relation either to each other or to the whole; they have no place and they do not know how to act.

There soon follows a long passage to the effect that all Shelley's life, though he did not know her, Emilia was "the loadstar of my one desire," "this soul out of my soul," and "the veiled Divinity" of his world.

And then he invites her to "fly" with him beyond the walls that never yet constrained true love:

> Say, my heart's sister, wilt thou sail with me?
> Our bark is as an albatross, whose nest
> Is a far Eden of the purple East . . .[131]

Though Shelley was not an admirer of Biblical religion, he nevertheless had Eden on his program. In *A Defense of Poetry*, he says that "The freedom of women produced the poetry of sexual love. Love became a religion . . . and a paradise was created as out of the wrecks of Eden."[132] That is easy talk if one does not take seriously the meaning of Eden in either Biblical or English poetic tradition. Even so, if one is going to reenter Eden by the "religion" of sexual love, then it will help if one can convince oneself that sexual love is not physical but spiritual. And Shelley's Eden is spiritual enough: "It is an isle 'twixt Heaven, Air, Earth, and Sea. . . ."[133] There the lovers will "rise, and sit, and walk together," enjoying the intellectual delights of books, music, and natural beauty—until:

> Our breath shall intermix, our bosoms bound,
> And our veins beat together; and our lips

With other eloquence than words, eclipse
The soul that burns between them . . .[134]

Well, that is spirituality with a fever! It can only remind the es-
tranged lover how miserable he is in the real world, and the passage ends in one of his sinking spells: "I pant, I sink, I tremble, I
expire!"[135]

This is a consuming passion because it is an egotistical passion. The egotism of the poem is omnivorous. The lady, one
feels, is only fodder. Shelley exalts, idealizes, deifies her—the
better to envelop her in the mist of his self-exalting emotion. She
is never in any sense *presented* in the poem, which only tells us
how grandly Shelley feels about her.

That this poem begins with a repudiation of marriage seems
to license everything that is wrong with it, for marriage is the
earthly form of love that gives love its place and work and provides for the good care of *both* bodies and souls. Marriage,
among other things that it is, is a way of saying that though love
does differ from "gold and clay," it must not be *divided* from
them, for if it is, then love, gold, and clay, all three, become displaced, aimless, and dangerous. Marriage takes love out of the
mind and places it responsibly in the world.

I believe that there is a widespread assumption that the Romantic Movement was a movement toward nature, away from
the alleged rationalism, formalism, and anthropocentricity of a
poet such as Pope. Hazlitt seems to doubt that this is true, in general, of the Romantic poets. It is certainly untrue, in general, of
Shelley, who constantly interposes his ego between himself and
nature. In his poems the creatures of nature, like Emilia Viviani,
are characteristically used as properties of scenes and landscapes that are predeterminately inward and ideal. His skylark
is introduced into its poem as a "spirit," not a bird. It is a sym-
bol—what *he* wants it to be—of ideal joy. More specifically, the
skylark is not Shelley, but is more joyful, less thwarted in love
and in thought, more harmoniously mad, than he is. His language has lost its designative power, and cannot present or re-

spect the bird as such. I do not mean that it is inherently wrong to speak of a bird as a spirit, but to see it *only* as a spirit is to fail to see it as a bird. It is hard not to feel that nature would be safer with Pope, who felt and cared for its materiality, than with so compulsive a spiritualizer as Shelley.

The point, which Shelley's great poetic mentors insist upon, is that things cannot be so parceled out. Things in nature cohere, and humans rightly belong to that coherence, but on the peculiarly human condition that if they are to belong to it, and not destroy it (and themselves), they must consciously join it. They must accept it humbly as a gift at once natural and divine, and they must be materially and practically responsible for it. Sexuality and fertility are natural and humans participate in them naturally, but if they are to be human "goods," humans must also participate in them responsibly. In Spenser, in Shakespeare, in Milton, the obligation is invariably double: inward and outward, upward and downward. Spenser's *Epithalamion* is a far more wholehearted love poem than *Epipsychidion* because it is sufficiently complex, *both* spiritual and physical, *both* heavenly and earthly, *both* joyful and responsible. Shelley tries to exalt sexual love simply by spiritualizing it—and makes a shambles of it, for which he characteristically pities *himself*.

This poem fails altogether because it is altogether unbelievable. The "suspension of disbelief," I think, requires that, although a poem may not be true for us, we must feel the possibility that it is true for *someone* other than the poet; we must sense that there is somewhere a common ground between the mind of the poet and other minds. *Epipsychidion* puts us off pretty quickly by the awareness that we cannot believe it except by fooling ourselves. It is full of overstated emotion, private fantasy, confusion, self-praise, and self-pity—all of which divide an individual from any common ground of experience or culture. And this problem is further aggravated by Shelley's assertion in the poem's behalf that "to a certain . . . class it must ever remain incomprehensible, from a defect of a common organ of perception for the ideas of which it treats."[136] An intelligent reader will resent this condescension, and refuse to be intimidated.

Why, then, is it not possible to ignore Shelley? There are two good reasons.

The first is that sometimes, as in *Adonais*, he is a superb poet. In that poem, except for the four stanzas in which he indecorously praises and pities himself, he is as sublime as he wanted to be. Except in those stanzas, his egotism is restrained and his mind steadied by his sense of the occasion, by elegiac tradition, by his great technical power; perhaps as a consequence, the creatures of nature appear in this poem simply as themselves, in their own particularity and right; real nature and natural process are here:

> The ants, the bees, the swallows reappear;
> Fresh leaves and flowers deck the dead Seasons' bier;
> The amorous birds now pair in every brake,
> And build their mossy homes in field and brere;
> And the green lizard, and the golden snake,
> Like unimprisoned flames, out of their trance awake.
> . . . .
> The leprous corpse, touched by this spirit tender,
> Exhales itself in flowers of gentle breath;
> Like incarnations of the stars, when splendour
> Is changed to fragrance, they illumine death
> And mock the merry worm that wakes beneath . . .[137]

Shelley is most natural where he is most traditional; those birds were pairing also in Chaucer and Spenser.

The other reason we cannot ignore Shelley, cannot *afford* to ignore him, is that we have so fully inherited his faults: his egotism, his rebellious individualism, his compulsion to divide reality into discrete parcels, his inclination to make a place of the mind.

The last of those faults seems to me to be the greatest and to be either the cause or the necessary condition of the others. Shelley thought to divide the mind from the material world for the protection of the mind. He thought the world of the mind to be so "high" that he could not bear to have it corrupted by materiality—and so, oddly, his thought parallels the "other-worldly, the puritanical," strain of that Christianity he so despised. But his division of mind from materiality only makes two separate realms of *mind*, as the outcome shows. For "mechanists" and "political economists," engineers, physicists, financiers, and war makers all live in *their* minds, too. When Hazlitt said of Wordsworth that "the image is lost in the sentiment . . . ,"[138] he might as well have been speaking of Shelley. When Yeats said of Shelley that "his landscapes are vaporized and generalized by his purpose . . . ," and that he was (therefore?) "the tyrant of his own being,"[139] he might as well have been speaking of scientists, industrialists, developers, rulers, and military leaders of our own time. Chesterton saw the culmination of Shelley's division of mind and world in the economics of "modern commerce," and he understood its essential fraudulence:

> They [American advertisers] are always telling us that the success of modern commerce depends on creating an atmosphere, on manufacturing a mentality, on assuming a point of view. In short, they insist that their commerce is not merely commercial, or even economic or political, but purely psychological. I hope they will go on saying it; for then some day everybody may suddenly see that it is true.
>
> For the success of big shops and such things really is psychology . . . or, in other words, nightmare. It is not real and, therefore, not reliable.[140]

The loving attentiveness to natural things, going all the way back through the poets of our tradition, gave nature a way of speaking to culture, of speaking *back* to and correcting culture. To turn poetry (or, for that matter, religion) wholly toward "the eternal, the infinite, and the one," and wholly away from "time and place and number," is to participate in what Dryden saw as a process of uncontrollable rebellion and individuation—schizogenesis, not as a form of growth, but as a wasting disease. Once the care of the material world is assigned exclusively to certain minds and to certain *parts* of minds, then the ability to care for it is lost. The mind's purpose generalizes and vaporizes the landscape; materials become "raw materials" or "natural resources" or "subject matter." And it is the mind, not the body, whose appetite for material things is insatiable. From about Shelley's time the world—for artists, scientists, industrialists, and consumers alike—has not been God-centered, nature-centered, or human-centered; it has been human-mind-centered. Hugh Kenner notes this change with approval in finding Ezra Pound more backward than R. Buckminster Fuller, who said that the source of all wealth is "the minds of world man.' " Pound, according to Mr. Kenner, failed to understand industrialization:

> Always he referred wealth to the soil—the sun, the grass, the sheep, the olive trees—in a time when increasingly its source was the mind. It may one day seem that he missed, in his isolation, the major historical event of his time, the *de facto* transfer of the basis of capital from matter to understanding. . .[141]

But the world that is human-mind-centered will tend to become money-centered; money is not material, nor can it reliably *stand for* material things; it is one of the purest of *ideas*, an abstraction of quantitative value. This abstract wealth will turn upon and destroy material wealth. Soil, sun, grass, sheep, and trees cannot stand against it. And this Pound saw and said plainly and memorably:

> With usura hath no man a house of good stone
> each block cut smooth and well fitting
> that design might cover their face . . .
> . . . .
> with usura, sin against nature,
> is thy bread ever more of stale rags
> is thy bread dry as paper,
> with no mountain wheat, no strong flour . . .
>
> . . . .

WITH USURA
wool comes not to market
sheep bringeth no gain with usura
Usura is a murrain, usura
blunteth the needle in the maid's hand . . .

. . . .

Usura rusteth the chisel
It rusteth the craft and the craftsman
It gnaweth the thread in the loom
None learneth to weave gold in her pattern . . .

. . . .

Usura slayeth the child in the womb
It stayeth the young man's courting
It hath brought palsey to bed, lyeth
between the young bride and her bridegroom . . .[142]

Usury is the perfect triumph of mind over matter, allowing a false value to reproduce by a kind of parthenogenesis, increasing the consumptive (and destructive) power of people who own money, destroying the productive power of people who own soil, grass, sheep, and trees, shops, and tools. When the distinction of values between money and property is lost, then the dominant political oppositions become merely quarrels about how to divide the spoils accruing from the abuse and destruction of property. At the end of his long study of Pound, Mr. Kenner condescends to him because he saw too late the mind-as-wealth ideology of R. Buckminster Fuller: "So he aged, a relic." I am Mr. Kenner's admirer and debtor, but I think he was wrong here. Hazlitt saw the wickedness of this intellectual imperialism, and sanely described and condemned it:

> wherever an intense activity is given to any one faculty, it necessarily prevents the due and natural exercise of others. Hence all those professions or pursuits where the mind is exclusively occupied with the ideas of things as they exist in the imagination or understanding, as they call for the exercise of intellectual activity, and not as they are connected with practical good or evil, must check the genial expansion of the moral sentiments and social affections; must lead to a cold and dry abstraction, as they are found to suspend the animal functions and relax the bodily frame. Hence the complaint of the want of

natural sensibility and constitutional warmth of attachment in those persons who have been devoted to the pursuit of any art or science,—of their restless morbidity of temperament, and indifference to everything that does not furnish an occasion for the display of their mental superiority and the gratification of their vanity.[143]

In a human-mind-centered world, knowledge and ideas become merchandise and are sold in and by universities, which is evident both in the current academic trade in money-valued degrees and in the growing number of academic "services" to corporations. This does not mean that real values can be traded for false ones; the false ones *destroy* the real ones. Universities that sell ideas must sell destructive ideas; they cannot sell good ones, because as soon as they become willing to sell bad ones, they *have* no good ones.

When mind predominates by the satanic principles of rebellion and division, then the individual is "liberated"; all his or her wants and wishes are made equal to any other wants and wishes and assume the status of legitimate values or goals. The usefulness of this state of affairs to an economy based upon consumption is obvious. So is its usefulness to an intellectual class organized on the plan of the modern university and believing, under the rubric of Progress, that thought should be specialized and "free." Thus in its economic and scientific aspects, the satanic rebellion has attained to orthodoxy. But its political and social aspects are anathema to a plutocratic ruling class, which intends to protect the blocks of wealth built up by the liberated rebels of science and industry. This is the ruinous contradiction underlying present-day American "conservatism." For the present economy to thrive or even survive, it is necessary for the great majority of the people to have exorbitant or inordinate wants, to expect to get what they want, and to feel that they have a "right" to get it. But to the bewilderment of "conservatives," this remorseless wanting cannot be confined to the "marketplace"; it is a general disorder, not anarchic but chaotic.

All this, of course, lies between the bridegroom and the bride. The economy "grows" upon the destruction of marriages, families, and households—the physical pursuit of sexual fantasy being one of the recognized driving forces of the market—which our "conservatives" have the luxury of both abetting and lamenting. Where, then, is the new Paradise to be made by the triumph of industrial technology? It does not exist. The poetic prophecies of it, from Wordsworth's "Steamboats, Viaducts, and Railways" to Whitman's "A Passage to India" only add new absurdity to old impossibility.

"Love makes all things equal," Shelley said, but so does this individual "liberation," which is implicit in Shelley's idea of love. However false or impossible such egalitarianism may be, it can still be adopted as a rule of behavior and have an influence. What it does immediately is pull down and shatter the hierarchies both of creatures and of values, and this cannot happen without producing a state of profound disorder. For when hierarchy is destroyed, not just in false or unjust *instances*, but *in principle*, then all the kinds of things, and therefore all things, are by definition displaced. It is the hierarchical principle of the Chain of Being that makes it all-inclusive; Creation is not so bountiful and various as it is because life is copious, but because it is orderly, full of places where an abounding diversity of creatures can be at home. By definition, the Chain of Being can exclude no *kind*; like Eden and the Ark, it affords room to every species of living thing. If all the kinds were equal, all places would be in dispute, to be contended for. The result would be a free-for-all, which in turn could only result either in a restoration of hierarchy or in total annihilation, for the most powerful kind would either destroy *all* the less powerful, and so eventually destroy itself, or it would repect their places in an order which both keeps them alive and implies their right to live.

Once the hierarchies of creatures and values are overturned and all things are equal, the past is lost and the present undermined, for then nothing can have a lasting value. The ferocious equation between abstraction and materiality will be free to establish itself, after which nothing can exist that cannot finally be "equalled" by enough money or power to destroy it. Nothing is then worth as much as what may replace it: spouse or household or public building or work of art or farm or wilderness. To the modern consumer, to the economic or intellectual or artistic puritan, to the technological romantic, to the progressive politician, any given thing is the first of a series of increasingly better things. Everything is a steppingstone or foothold. Natural and human households and communities are destroyed and local history uprooted by corporate or governmental "development," because development, being forever new, is worth more than anything old; people are replaced by machines, because when people have no place in any respected order, they are seen as inferior to machines; community is replaced by law, because when all wants and wishes are equal, law must be externalized. Though this process of rebellion and division will always claim the goals of personal liberation and self-fulfillment, its ultimate value is money value and its ultimate power is police power.

Amid the welter of contentions and oppressions that inevitably follow the destruction of any comprehensive idea of order, the ideas of "autonomy" and "autotelism" have been invoked as protections of valued things: creatures, people, and works of art have all at various times and under various stresses been said to exist for their own sakes. But this is a forlorn and dangerous defense. Nothing is meaningful or valuable alone; to assign meaning and value to anything alone is, I believe, what used to be understood as "idolatry." Nothing can be its own context. Meaning and value are not generated by parts, but are conferred by the whole. The only safe contexts are, first, natural order and, second, a human culture formed in respect for natural order.

The loss of the hierarchic principle did not, as some have supposed, bring humans closer to nature. It was only after the Chain of Being had apparently disappeared as a way of thought that poets began to feel exiled from nature and to yearn toward it. Only then did they begin to envy skylarks, wish to fade into the forest with nightingales, or think that they "could turn and live with animals." And this yearning has little to do with the imaginative evocations of animal life that one finds in the Book of Job, say, or in Milton's images of the Creation. It has little to do with the animals' grace of form or movement or with the harmoniousness of natural neighborhoods and households but involves unlikely human assumptions about nature, imposed upon it: the notion, for instance, that animals are always happy, not feelingly involved in chance, suffering, and mortality. At times this wish to escape into nature is no such thing at all, but rather a poetic way of wishing to be a spirit. All this, it seems to me, comes from the loss of any sound understanding either of animals or of humans. Humans cannot live with animals, if that implies, as I think it usually does, living *as* animals, and remain human; and it is only by remaining human—that is, by the acceptance and the proper use of the human powers—that they can understand, respect, and preserve the animals.

The notion of romantic poets that they would like to turn and live with or as animals is a fantasy that has its counterpart in the notion of scientific and technological romantics that they will eventually turn and live with or as gods. Both notions would have been understood by Spenser or Shakespeare or Milton or Pope as sinful—not because either turning is possible, but because *neither* is. The evil of such notions is that they mislead us dangerously about our own nature; they are illusions that corrupt and debase our humanity.

Implicit in the Chain of Being is the idea that creatures are protected in their various kinds, not by equality, but by difference; and that if humans are responsibly observant of the differences between themselves and the angels above them and the animals below, they will act with respect, restraint, and benevolence toward the subordinate creatures; this is their duty toward the subordinate creatures, and it is part of, inseparable from, their duty to the higher creatures and to God. If one is properly humble before Heaven, then one's earthly conduct must be properly careful and restrained; if one loves the Creator, one must love His creatures which, after all, live by His will and by sharing His life. When humans keep their proper place in the Chain, the connections are unbroken from the microorganisms to God. When humans abdicate their proper place, either by pride or self-debasement, they blaspheme God and brutalize nature. So Pope argued, and he spoke for the great poets who preceded him.

When the differences between humans and animals, humans and angels become unclear, one result, I think, is that the difference between biological creatures and machines becomes unclear. That would account for the occurrence of the power-failure image in Auden's elegy for Yeats. It would account for the general acceptance of the industrial substitution of machines for people, for the application of factory organization to farming and education, for the ideal of "control" in politics and applied science, for the concepts of total government and total war. All this suggests that having a place, having a definition and limits, belonging to a kind unlike other kinds, may not be so confining as might at first appear, but is, rather, the condition upon which we truly are set free, admitted to the Creation and the community of the creatures.

The Chain of Being was abandoned as a way of understanding because it seemed to be invalidated by new knowledge and by the experimental method. Nothing above the human link could be proved, and belief, for many of the "best minds," became contingent upon proof and explanation. At the same time, human destiny came to be conceived, not as a pilgrimage to God, but as a ladder or a rising road that humans ascended by knowledge and will in an unending "progress," which assumed no limit on human merit and no need for divine grace; to be a human was to be a potential or a growing god. From this point of view, the *Paradiso* was superstition and bad astronomy. Below the human link, new proofs and theories disrupted the old arrangements, and suggested moreover that the lower part of the Chain was also a ladder, up which the creatures were all evolving. If so, then the accounts of the Creation in Genesis and *Paradise Lost* were superstition and bad biology.

And so all the creatures were, and are, freed from their places into confusion. It is as though Noah's Ark has just landed and opened its doors. Every creature is hesitating, not knowing where to go or what to do. The grazers have not grazed; the predators have killed no prey; the birds have not flown; the lizards are perhaps waiting to turn into birds. And none are more free or more confused than the humans. Where do *they* belong? What must they do? Must they kill and eat these very creatures that they have saved? Or should they eat these plants or these fruits that have been saved also—not by them—perhaps for the animals? What else is there to eat but other creatures, none exactly belonging to any human? What rights do they have? What restitutions are required? What is their *place*? The situation is full of danger, not least that someone will eat the last seed or the last pregnant female of some species. Obviously a kind of manners, a kind of *courtesy* is required. Things must be respected according to their degrees. First things must be recognized and put first. It will be dangerous to do anything until it is understood what is proper to do. The animals will hesitate, one assumes, only long enough to accustom their eyes to the light and to feel the prompting of instinct, but the humans yearn for law. They yearn for law, I think, because they sense that law is probably what they are up against, and that it is law that *they* do not instinctively know, but must learn.

In this dilemma the romantic program has little to offer. The romantic mind is a mind apart. It conceives of itself as divided from nature and superior to it, not as stranded with it on the same mountaintop. To the romantic poet, nature is a stock of symbols and subjects, to be observed (better if from a certain distance), yearned toward, worshipped for the sake of the unseen power behind it. To the romantic scientist, nature is a stock of natural resources to be used however seems necessary to further the human ascent toward a godlike autonomy and control.

Both, in their different ways, propose that a new Eden, an earthly Paradise, can be made solely by "the discerning intellect of Man:"

> Paradise, and groves
> Elysian, Fortunate Fields—like those of old
> Sought in the Atlantic Main—why should they be
> A history only of departed things,
> Or a mere fiction of what never was?[144]

That there might be laws of nature that are absolute and that imply human laws also absolute has not been thought a considerable or a tolerable possibility by the romantic party from Wordsworth to the technological visionaries of our own time. They have disdained the possibility that these laws imply a limiting definition of humanity. That they imply and enforce the practical considerations of propriety and right livelihood, the romantics have apparently never dreamed.

The Chain of Being is not, in itself, a law. It is a way of understanding things seen or felt to be true. But it is full of the implication of law, which poets as late as Pope did not hesitate to make explicit. It is a description of the possibility of law, both true and false. And whatever may be its shortcomings from an experimental point of view, it defines the human place in the order of creatures with great moral exactitude. It answers the dilemma of Noah and his family by providing them a possibility and a way of thinking; it permits them to think thoughts that can motivate and measure and regulate acts. Perhaps most important, it sets up an authority that is outside and above individual intelligence, *any* individual intelligence; the laws immanent in it are therefore neither arbitrary nor tyrannical. Humans are thus spared the insufferable bewilderment and anxiety of having to respond to a dangerous predicament by their own rules.

It would be a mistake to assume, because the Chain of Being is so manifestly present in writings, that it is only a literary or philosophical artifact. Long before it became explicit in literature, the moral implications of the human place in it were well understood. It is easy to suppose that the roots of the idea go back to whatever events first differentiated humans from animals. From the beginning of human life, we must have been dependent upon the perception that humans are neither gods nor beasts. That perception and its moral implications must have preceded Homer and the Bible. It was not just a way for humans to recognize themselves as such, but was itself one of the vitals of their identity. And down at least through the work of Pope, one of the necessary services of the poets was to reunderstand and renew this idea, reimagine its human embodiments and catastrophes, and keep it alive. Poetry, then, was—and it may be—a part of the necessary cultural means by which we preserve our union, the possibility of harmony, with the natural world and "higher law."

In light of that history and that possibility, Wordsworth's statement of his purpose as a poet comes as a shock. He sang, he said,

> Of the individual Mind that keeps her own
> Inviolate retirement, subject there
> To Conscience only, and the law supreme
> Of that Intelligence which governs all . . .[145]

It is not clear, at least from the immediate context, how Wordsworth proposed to learn the "law supreme," whether by intuition or interpretation or both, but these lines appear to bring him to the same problem that Dryden had come to at the end of *Religio Laici*: he affirms the existence both of individual conscience and of a supreme intelligence, but he has affirmed no earthly thing between them that can correct his understanding of either or bring the two into harmony. The disembodied individual mind is seen as occupying the space or perhaps the difference between the extremes of private conscience and supreme intelligence, also disembodied. The mind is not only individual here, but solitary; this difference or middle space is both natureless and cultureless.

To mediate between conscience and supreme intelligence is probably an impossible task for the individual mind alone; Dryden saw and accepted this as a problem, but Wordsworth apparently sees no difficulty in it at all. The "manifesto" at the end of *The Recluse*, from which I have been quoting, contains one of the strangest of invocations:

> Urania, I shall need
> Thy guidance, or a greater Muse, if such
> Descend to earth or dwell in highest heaven!
> For I must tread on shadowy ground, must sink
> Deep—and, aloft ascending, breathe in worlds
> To which the heaven of heavens is but a veil.
> All strength—all terror, single or in bands,
> That ever was put forth in personal form—
> Jehovah—with his thunder, and the choir
> Of shouting Angels, and the empyreal thrones—
> I pass them unalarmed. Not Chaos, not
> The darkest pit of lowest Erebus,
> Nor aught of blinder vacancy, scooped out
> By help of dreams—can breed such fear and awe
> As fall upon us often when we look
> Into our Minds, into the Mind of Man—
> My haunt, and the main region of my song.[146]

"The Mind of Man," then is so copious as to contain the universe with some room to spare above and below. He can "pass" Jehovah, the Angels, and empyrean Heaven "unalarmed," and he can descend past Hell and Chaos without much need of help from the Muse. What fills him with fear and awe is to enter "the Mind of Man." That sets him praying—and it well ought to, considering the arrogance of that mind as represented here and remembering how humbly Dante invoked the Muses and Apollo on his own comparatively short journey. It is hard to tell which is greater here, Wordsworth's spiritual presumptuousness or his poetic impudence. And what are we to make of the proposition that a mind so large can at the same time be so small as to enter itself with awe and fear?

This mind, moreover, has no problems with "the external World." It is simply "exquisitely . . . fitted" to it. When the two are "blended," Paradise will be renewed. ("For this purpose,"

Hazlitt says, "I think several things necessary which are impossible.")[147] Some little difficulty is anticipated with humanity's "madding passions," "solitary anguish," and its sorrow "within the walls of cities," but (the Muse aiding) "authentic comment" will be given to these, and so the poet will not be "downcast or forlorn." Besides, his real aim is to receive the "prophet Spirit," and dream of things to come.

It would be hard to overestimate the silliness of this mind, and yet we are obliged to see it as a mind coming to power, possessed of a history and a future. It has behind it all in human arrogance and ambition that speaks in Milton's Satan's determination that "The mind is its own place. . . ." Ahead of it, it has all the propaganda and the works of the scientific romanticism that have accompanied the industrial revolution. For if the poetic individual mind can pass unalarmed the heaven of heavens and the whole spiritual order of the universe, why cannot the scientific individual mind do so as well?

It was in opposition to such minds that Pope's mind was set:

Go, wond'rous creature! mount where Science guides,
Go, measure earth, weigh air, and state the tides;
Instruct the planets in what orbs to run,
Correct old Time, and regulate the Sun;
Go, soar with Plato to th'empyreal sphere,
To the first good, first perfect, and first fair;
Or tread the mazy round his follow'rs trod,
And quitting sense call imitating God . . .

. . . .

Go, teach Eternal Wisdom how to rule—
Then drop into thyself, and be a fool![148]

To return from Wordsworth's invocation to those chastening lines of Pope is to return to what is sanest in our tradition and in our nature.

Wordsworth's mind and the mind he speaks for in the invocation are, of course, not always the same. Hazlitt saw his egotism, and

rightly condemned it. And it is easy to see the egotistical Wordsworth as ancestor to what is worst in Shelley, and in us. But there
are times when Wordsworth's mind is sounder, sweeter, and
more modest, and at these times his mind is turned toward the
shepherds, farmers, and other working country people whom he
knew well and loved. In *Michael*, for instance, one does not feel
anywhere the cold breath of the egotist.

In *Michael* and in the remembrances of shepherds in *The Prelude*, Wordsworth's affection and understanding are wholehearted, and these people seem to offer his mind its most authentic means of apprehending places, both in their physical presence and in their "Genius":

> There, 'tis the shepherd's task the winter long
> To wait upon the storms: of their approach
> Sagacious, into sheltering coves he drives
> His flock, and thither from the homestead bears
> A toilsome burden up the craggy ways,
> And deals it out, their regular nourishment
> Strewn on the frozen snow.[149]

And there is an understanding of the possibility of a practical
harmony between people and nature that recalls the *Epistle to
Burlington*:

>   the sun and the sky,
> The elements and seasons as they change,
> Do find a worthy fellow-labourer there—
> Man free, man working for himself, with choice
> Of time, and place, and object; by his wants,
> His comforts, native occupations, cares,
> Cheerfully led to individual ends
> Or social, and still followed by a train
> Unwooed, unthought-of even—simplicity,
> And beauty, and inevitable grace.[150]

But something is wrong in the feeling of these passages, and
one feels it in the language. Why should the shepherd be "saga-
cious" of the approaching storm? Why cannot the sheep's "reg-

ular nourishment" be called "hay"? Why must the free man be
followed by a "train"? Those lines say only that he is "followed
by unwooed / Beauty, simplicity, and grace." Is Wordsworth
padding his lines? (He could generally do with fewer.) Is he af-
fecting some elegance of diction? Or is he unconsciously apolo-
gizing for the "lowness" of these people? The hint of unwitting
condescension is stronger when he generalizes them into "man /
Ennobled outwardly before my sight";[151] there is more than a
hint of it when he hopes, as though doubting, that they have in
them "attendant gleams / Of soul-illumination"[152] or asserts,
like Thomas Gray, that many of them are "Poets that are sown /
By Nature . . . Yet wanting the accomplishment of verse . . . ,"[153]
as though their own work did not involve the intricacy of knowledge, the formidable skills, and the beauty that we find fully
credited at last in the work of Thomas Hardy.

The impulse to know and honor these people is nevertheless
authentic in Wordsworth, and it is also traditional, for one of the
insistently recurring themes, not just of literature but of human
life, is the necessary meeting of high company with low company, high culture with low culture. Poetry may and perhaps
should exalt language, but it also must return to "the very language of men"[154]—a departure and return that it has made
many times. It departs by an aspiration that we understand as
belonging to our nature. It returns because of an apprehension,
perhaps belonging to the nature of poetry, that language can be
carried *too* high. It can be so exalted as to fail to touch and designate and mean in this world.

Thus in the history of poetry and in the work of some individual poets we find a kind of rhythm of aspiration and descent, of
departure and homecoming. This homecoming is always a renewal of both art and earthly vision; it is a return both to "the
very language of men" and to their very world. The homecoming
at times involves sorrow, for its direction, after all, is downward;
but it invariably involves relief, as all homecomings must. Both
the sorrow and the relief are in Milton's invocation in Book VII

of *Paradise Lost*; he has been singing of Heavenly events, and now he asks his Muse to descend:

> Up led by thee
> Into the Heav'n of Heav'ns I have presum'd,
> An Earthly Guest . . .
> . . . .
>
> Return me to my Native Element:
> Lest from this flying Steed unrein'd, (as once
> *Bellerophon*, though from a lower Clime)
> Dismounted, on th' *Aleian* Field I fall
> Erroneous there to wander and forlorn.
> . . . .
>
> Standing on Earth, not rapt above the Pole,
> More safe I Sing with mortal voice, unchang'd
> To hoarse or mute, though fall'n on evil days . . .[155]

And this is a movement not across the supposed divisions of Heaven and Earth or body and soul, but across another dichotomy both more authentic and more significant.

The earlier poets did often fall into the body-soul or matter-mind division that was to be so ruinous when poetic and industrial romanticism made a program of it. Sometimes they affirm this division, regretting or repudiating the soul's "imprisonment" in the body and the material world—feelings that are, surely, ancient. And yet it could be argued that when they are truest to their religion and their poetic tradition, they understand that this division is, in fact, impossible: that body and soul delight as well as suffer in each other and are in a sense each other's crisis; that to attempt or pretend to divide them is foolhardy, dangerous, and evil. The real task is to bring them into unity or harmony, and this is to be done by the cultivation of virtues, both practical and spiritual, which are enjoined upon us by what are called divine commandments or moral laws, and which may be understood as a set of instructions for preserving our place and our places and ourselves in them.

There are two other dichotomies that they recognized and accepted as not resolvable: that of good and evil and that of nature or wildness and human nature or domesticity. The double concept of place that I have been defining and illustrating from the poets can be understood as explaining the difference and the division between good and evil. If we understand this concept of place carefully and fully enough, we can say simply that to be in place is good and to be out of place is evil, for where we are with respect to our place both in the order of things and on earth is the definition of our whereabouts with respect to God and our fellow creatures.

The dichotomy of wildness and domesticity is a matter more complex and difficult for, unlike good and evil, wildness and domesticity, from the human point of view, are not entirely separable except as concepts and moreover are dependent upon one another. They are not interchangeable; they cannot *be* each other, but they cannot get along without each other. They are different, that is, not like good and evil, but like male and female;[156] they are different, but not divided.

This is the difference that Wordsworth moves across, and moves poetry across, in his best poems and passages on nature and country people. But this difference comprehends several subdifferences that are analogous: individuality and community, sexuality and marriage, fertility and agriculture, inspiration and poetry, for examples; and so we can say also that Milton moves across it when he moves his poem from the purely inspired or purely imaginary passages in Heaven back to earth where his singing will, he prays, be still inspired but now also *knowledgeable*. We can say also that any poet crosses this difference who transforms inspiration into a poem, for inspiration is as wild as a forest in the sense that, as poets' invocations testify, humans do not make it, whereas a poem is a domestic artifact which, if not made by a human, would not exist. Poetry's artificiality, its technical and formal difficulty, informs us of our *human* nature, and, if we will be properly faithful and attentive to it, it will prevent us from presuming upon and abusing the source. The source of poetry, like the sources of all other domestic goods, is not our own. To draw upon it without falsifying or destroying it, we must become worthy of it.

The dualism of domestic and wild certainly involves opposition and tension, but from the domestic point of view it also involves dependence; domestic structures that shut out, ignore, or destroy their wild sources are therefore doomed. Likewise, any wildness within human power that is not allowed for and sanctioned by domestic structures is therefore doomed. The ideal, as poets from Homer to Pound have instructed us, is harmony: the domestic must be placed within the wild—for the wild must always be larger—with such studied and elegant propriety as to preserve *both*.

Pound is speaking in understanding of this essential propriety, as both man and poet, when he says:

> Pull down thy vanity, it is not man
> Made courage, or made order, or made grace . . .
> . . . .
> Learn of the green world what can be thy place
> In scaled invention or true artistry . . .[157]

It is vain to think either that the mind can *be* a place, or that the mind alone can *find* a proper place for itself or for us. It must look out of itself into the world.

One of the uses of poetry is to reveal and articulate and make and preserve the necessary connections between the domestic and the wild. It is one of the ways we may, with hope of return, get out of our minds (our own and other people's) into the world of creatures, forms, and powers that we did not make. Access to that world is sanity. To be trapped in one's own mind is insanity. To be trapped in another person's mind—by political or technological tyranny—is imprisonment. (To want to live, like a frontiersman, where one cannot see the smoke of one's neighbor's fire may be a kind of foolishness; it is not foolish to want to live beyond the radiation of one's neighbor's power plant.)

But to be trapped outside one's mind, in wildness unmitigated by a human culture that prepares us to be there, is the opposite kind of insanity. The first kind makes us lonely, anomalous, useless, and hopeless. The second makes us monstrous. To be trapped in the mind is to be like Shelley in his worst fits of self-pity. To be trapped outside is to be like Macbeth after the murder of Duncan. What is lost, either way, is essential knowledge, essential remembrance, essential restraint.

If human nature is double, then its two halves must meet and inform each other. This seems to be one of the oldest cultural themes. In primitive cultures, as in the earliest surviving documents of our own culture, the wilderness is understood as a necessary place of trial, initiation, or healing. An individual or a whole nation may be required to go into the wilderness and in that absence from home to learn or relearn something essential. That learning cleaves its way among differences. Devils and angels must be dealt with. Good and evil choices offer themselves in ways that cannot be escaped or ignored. The right path must be chosen among wrong paths, and there are sure penalties for error. In the process, the mind renews its grasp on what is worthy and is stripped of its dross.

At other times a similar movement is made, and to the same purpose, from high culture to low culture, as when a New England Transcendentalist goes to the woods to live in the rebuilt house of a pauper. The result, either way, is a renewed or corrected understanding of the dependence of human life on its unhuman sources, of the domestic on the wild.

The pastoral tradition is one of the carriers of this theme, and it is a tradition peculiarly well suited for bringing the two sides together, for it is, as we have it, a high-cultural means of reaching to low or rural culture and, through the low culture, to nature. One of the interests of pastoral poetry is to compare the courtier's life to the life of a shepherd or small farmer and to find in country life a standard by which to judge and reject or correct life at court. It is necessary to speak of this tradition with a good deal of caution, for our reading of most pastoral poets must answer to Dr. Johnson's fundamental stricture against "Lycidas": "We know that they never drove a field, and that they had no flocks to batten. . . ."[158] It is true that traditional pastoral poems must be suspected of being self-consciously artificial, full of conventional props and furnishings. It would be a mistake to suppose that courtiers like Ronsard and Spenser had much experience of the daily life of plowmen and shepherds. But it would be a mistake also to suppose that they knew as little of rural life as, say, most American politicians of our own time. Though it must be granted that pastoral tradition made possible a lot of poetical silliness about the idyllic lives of "simple people living close to nature," we must acknowledge also that it bears a certain indispensable truth and health.

The court poets turned to pastoral, I think, out of an authentic awareness that the high culture could be so high as to be false: the concerns and the trappings of wealth and power could distract people from their real interests, could cause them to value the wrong things, worry about the wrong things, and be dangerously ignorant of needs and lives fundamental to their good. A man of Spenser's robust intelligence would see the jeopardies of dependence and of needing too much. And so in Book VI of *The Faerie Queene* he brings Sir Calidore to the house of old Meliboe, a shepherd, with whose foster daughter, Pastorella, the knight falls in love. The high and the low are thus brought face to face—for the instruction, as is typical, of the high. Sir Calidore is the knight best suited for this encounter and this instruction, for he represents "Curtesie," the virtue of proper respect "To all of each degree, as doth behoue. . . ."[159] This "Curtesie" is not social etiquette, but all that is comprehended in the capability of decorous or ordinate behavior: knowing, in any place or company, what is proper to do, and how best to do it.

When Calidore commends "the happie life, / Which Shepheards lead,"[160] Meliboe gives the homily that one expects:

> If happie, then it is in this intent,
> That hauing small, yet doe I not complaine
> Of want, ne wish for more it to augment,

> But doe my self, with that I haue, content;
> So taught of nature, which doth litle need
> Of forreine helpes to lifes due nourishment:
> The fields my food, my flocke my rayment breed;
> No better doe I weare, no better doe I feed.[161]

The knight is thus taught by the shepherd who has been taught by nature, and the lesson is in the association of natural abundance with needing little "of forreine helpes," a lesson that is elaborated in *Comus*, and that can be elaborated almost endlessly in the local knowledges and skills that bind a culture preservingly to nature. John Todd is referring to this lesson, and reviving it, in his recognition of the need to adapt design to region: "Elegant solutions will be predicated upon the uniqueness of place."[162]

Meliboe's speech is homely, sensible, thoroughly traditional; not much is remarkable about it. It is, or at least it used to be, the standard parental advice: Stand on your own feet; be satisfied with what you can honorably earn. My argument, however, requires me to point out that Meliboe exactly contradicts Wordsworth's assumption that the individual mind is, in any immediate way, exquisitely fitted to the external world. Such a fitness is possible, but it comes neither from the mind nor from the world. It can come only from a human culture adequate to mediate between the two; it comes from the understanding of what is good. The individual mind, *thus* fitted to the world, "maketh good":

> For not that, which men couet most, is best,
> Nor that thing worst, which men do most refuse;
> But fittest is, that all contented rest
> With that they hold: each hath his fortune in his brest.

> It is the mynd, that maketh good or ill,
>   That maketh wretch or happie, rich or poore:
> For some, that hath abundance at his will,
>   Hath not enough, but wants in greatest store;
>   And other, that hath litle, askes no more,
>   But in that litle is both rich and wise.[163]

The human mind, then, within its limits, does have a power that is fearful and wonderful. It is not "its own place"; it cannot "make a Heav'n of Hell, a Hell of Heav'n"; it can do little "in itself." But depending on its ability or inability to see and preserve what is good, it *can* make a good place into a bad place or a bad place into a good place; it can be the disease of a place or its healing and health.

In *The Faerie Queen*, Book VI, the life of decent husbandry and frugal abundance, so fitting both to nature and to human nature, is set against an understanding of what is *not* fitting, for Meliboe once disdained "to follow sheep" and sought "further fortune:"

> leauing home, to roiall court I sought;
> Where I did sell my selfe for yearely hire,
> And in the Princes gardin daily wrought:
> There I beheld such vainenesse, as I neuer thought.[164]

To care properly for what is properly one's own is fitting. To exploit it—to sell oneself—is "vainenesse." This too is conventional in pastoral poetry, and native to common sense.

What does seem remarkable in Spenser's handling of this theme is that only after Calidore has himself begun to live the shepherd's life is he privileged to share Colin Clout's vision of the Graces "All raunged in a ring, and dauncing in delight."[165] And so in Spenser the high and the low, the wild and the domestic, the visionary and the practical, though certainly seen as different, are not divided and set at odds as they are in Shelley, but are necessary to each other, and open gracefully into each other.

The tendency of "cultured" people from Shelley's time to our own to make a simple dichotomy of high and low invariably leads to oversimplification of both and to ignorance of their close and often paradoxical connection. A clear implication of this traditional meeting of high and low is that the high is *made* high, or made worthy to be high, by low knowledge. If the worthies of the royal court understood the prostitution and the blasphemy of self-selling, they would be more fit to rule. It is certainly implied that David was worthy to be king, in part, by virtue of his having been a good shepherd, just as Odysseus is seen as kingly, in part, because he justly values his loyal swineherd Eumaios and so deserves his love. The high must descend to learn, not what it would choose to learn, but what is indispensable to high and low alike.

This descent, in both its political and its cultural aspects, is the subject of *As You Like It*, a play that is able to embody this pastoral theme without pastoral conventionality because Shakespeare had an authentic, immediate knowledge of country life; his characters are not, like Spenser's, conventional types, but are conceived in the particularity of place and calling.

All the characters in the play are brought down to better knowledge than they began with. There is now inevitably a "sophistication" (i.e., ignorance) that will look upon this descent as an "escape from the real world." This is apparently because the play has country people in it and takes place mainly in a forest, and most educated people now do not know much about either; they think that country people are stupid and that forests are places where one can be thoughtless and indulge in idle fancies. A "comedy" that takes place in a forest will, therefore, necessarily be frivolous. There is, of course, plenty of fun in *As You Like It*, and some frivolity too. Nobody gets killed, and the ending is happy, for the time being, for everybody. But a play whose themes are political corruption, family hatred, exile, courtship, marriage, and renewal of the human estate within nature, which in theme and (here and there) in diction echoes the New Testament and the Book of Job, and which has in it an old man named Adam, might reasonably be suspected of some measure of seriousness. And the play deals, in fact, with fundamental questions of propriety, of the real values of people, places, and things, of their proper relationships; and, if I am not mistaken, the Chain of Being stands beside it or behind it like a measuring rod.

The play begins with a series of images comparing people to beasts. Orlando is the ward of his older brother, Oliver, who hates him and has callously neglected his schooling. His brother's keeping, Orlando says, "differs not from the stalling of an ox[.] His horses are bred better. . . . I, his brother, gain nothing under him but growth, for the which his animals on his dunghill are as much bound to him as I."[166] In an angry exchange with Oliver, Orlando alludes to the parable of the Prodigal Son as a way both of describing his degradation and of asserting its injustice: "Shall I keep your hogs and eat husks with them? What prodigal portion have I spent that I should come to such penury?"[167] The quarrel ends in a rupture between the brothers. The old servant, Adam, loyal to Orlando, is called an "old dog" [168] by Oliver, and thus also alienated from the household.

To be treated like an animal is to be reduced, not to the status of an animal, but virtually to nothing, and this is the character of Orlando's despair:

> If I be foiled, there is but one shamed that was never gracious; if killed, but one dead that is willing to be so. I shall do my friends no wrong, for I have none to lament me; the world no injury, for in it I have nothing. Only in the world I fill up a place, which may be better supplied when I have made it empty.[169]

But Orlando defeats the wrestler who, at Oliver's instigation, meant to maim or kill him, wins the love of Rosalind, and, with Adam, goes into exile in the Forest of Arden.

Rosalind, the daughter of the exiled Duke Senior, is then almost immediately sent into exile herself by the reigning Duke Frederick, her uncle, who has "perforce" usurped the place of his brother. Disguised as a young man, accompanied by her loyal cousin Celia ("thou and I am one") and the clown, Touchstone, Rosalind too becomes an exile in Arden, where her father and a number of his retainers are known to be living "like the old Robin Hood of England."

The Forest of Arden, then, has become the gathering place of a number of people who in the briary "working-day world" have lost everything. Their destitution is not so great and tragic as Job's, but, like him, they have lost their lives as they were. The Forest, however, is not a place *of* loss; it is a place *beyond* loss, where they find their lives as they are—reduced to nothing by the standards of the working-day world, but, by the standards of nature, in the forest and in themselves, abounding. They lose their lives in order to find them, and that finding is the business of the last four acts.

To a modern reader, the speech of the exiled Duke at the beginning of Act II is apt to look like a piece of shallow optimism. But it is more sensible and more complicated than that, and to see that it is, we have only to recognize the traditions in which it is firmly set. The pastoral theme of a descent to true knowledge is stated plainly: "Are not these woods / More free from peril than the envious court?"[170]—which would be no more than pretty patter, maybe, if this were merely a "scenic" forest, but, as we learn later, there are dangerous beasts in it. The Duke's question carries the bitter insight that nothing in nature is so dangerous as a human made "unnatural" by vice. The seasons and the weather are not flatterers but forces of the natural world that strip away the falsely human and reveal the true: "these are counsellors / That feelingly persuade me what I am."[171] And the speech ends with these famous lines, which, if we are not careful, "sophistication" will persuade us to regard as "escapism" and a frivolous indulgence in the pathetic fallacy:

> And this our life, exempt from public haunt,
> Finds tongues in trees, books in running brooks,
> Sermons in stones, and good in everything.[172]

If we think that "the mind is its own place," these lines *are* frivolous; if we think that our place is in nature and that we are therefore obliged to learn from natural things, they are not frivolous, but true, and moreover traditional. They are exactly parallel to Meliboe's speech in *The Faerie Queene* (VI. IX. xx). They are in keeping with John Scotus Eriugena's belief that "the eternal Light reveals itself to the world in a twofold way: through Scripture and through creature."[173] They paraphrase Job 12:7–9:

> But ask now the beasts, and they shall teach thee; and the fowls of the air, and they shall tell thee:

Or speak to the earth, and it shall teach thee: and the fishes of the sea
  shall declare unto thee.
Who knoweth not in all these that the hand of the Lord hath wrought
  this?

And they end with a paraphrase of Genesis 1:31:

And God saw everything that he had made, and, behold, it was very
  good.

The only line in the Duke's speech that seems a little naive is
the fifth: "Here feel we not the penalty of Adam. . . ." There is a
sense in which this is so, and which is conformable to Scripture,
for they have returned to the Garden and to innocence by the
only legitimate way: by losing their lives as they were; in the loss
of worldly standing and possessions and the vices of the court,
they have become as little children. But in another sense the line
is untrue; the "golden world" in which they seem to be living is
illusory and temporary, for the exiles and the forest alike belong
to the fallen world, and, even as the Duke speaks, the old Adam
is on his way toward them. His arrival will start the play moving
toward the exiles' return to their worldly stations and responsibilities. This is a line, then, that the play must grow away from.

For the time being, the exiles are in the good natural world of
the forest, and their immediate problem is how to fit in. Shakespeare does not dwell on this problem, but he makes enough of it
to reveal that he saw it as a problem and to prevent us from ignoring it. The problem is a practical one and, for people with decent sympathies, not perfectly solvable: even this "innocent" life
in the forest must be lived at the expense of fellow creatures. The
Duke's next speech states the problem:

Come, shall we go and kill us venison?
And yet it irks me the poor dappled fools,
Being native burghers of this desert city,
Should, in their own confines, with forkèd heads
Have their round haunches gored.[174]

The Duke assumes that he has a proper place in nature, entitling
him to a proper use of other creatures for his sustenance. The

propriety of this use, I assume, is vouchsafed by his sympathy. A man who cares for his fellow creatures will not be profligate or "riotous" in his use of them.

Against the Duke's attitude is set that of "the melancholy Jaques," who thinks that the Duke and his companions

> Are mere usurpers, tyrants, and what's worse
> To fright the animals and to kill them up
> In their assigned and native dwelling place.[175]

This sympathy of Jaques is mere self-indulgence, an egalitarianism that can be the principle of no action. Jaques' feelings "go out" to animals as readily as to people, or more readily, but bind him to neither and are useless to both.

The play thus proposes three ways of coming to terms with the fallen world: the way of ambition, followed by the wicked brothers, which attempts a willful restoration of a Paradise in which individual desires are appeased; the way of Jaques who stands self-righteously aloof, indulging his sensitivities; and the way of the play itself, which moves between the extremes of abusive ambition and feckless sentimentality toward self-knowledge, true companionship, and "settled low content." This third way is the way of a this-worldly grace, which leads, not to a vision of the Graces dancing, but to a sort of dance pattern of marriages and reconciliations, which bring the wild energies of nature and sexuality to a proper domestication within the traditional bounds of human nature and which thus reconcile Heaven and Earth:

> Then is there mirth in heaven
> When earthly things made even
>   Atone together.[176]

The first scene of Act II is the needle's eye of the play. If we can pass through it without looking at its whereabouts in the world and in its tradition, then we will see the play as an escape from thought, "savoring more of the world of pleasant fancy than the world of strong imagination";[177] if we pass through it, seeing where we are, we must see the play as a parable, full of thought and strongly imagined (which, of course, does not prevent us from seeing it as a comedy).

The forest, unlike the court, is a circumstance in which humans appear as fully human, not as functions or functionaries of governmental power. If Shakespeare's exiles needed the forest—and if *we* need it—this is why. The forest provides the play an elemental setting, which transforms what at court would be mere civilities to a profound and feeling eloquence, not the etiquette of people who feel obliged to defer to one another, but the true courtesy of people who have understood the need to love one another:

> Welcome. Set down your venerable burden
> And let him feed.[178]

But the forest, though it is a wild place, is not understood as a place where humans become wild or "savage." It is the place where their real nature, their culture or human nature, is restored to them. Orlando comes into it bearing, in the figure of the old Adam, the whole history of the human race in the fallen world. He at first is made "savage," not by the forest, but by his mistaken fear that the exiles are "savage." He finds instead that he has come to a place of peace, more brotherly than his brother's house. And this peace is the gift of the best of his own culture, recovered in the forest:

> True is it that we have seen better days,
> And have with holy bell been knolled to church,
> And sat at good men's feasts, and wiped our eyes
> Of drops that sacred pity hath engend'red;
> And therefore sit you down in gentleness,
> And take upon command what help we have
> That to your wanting may be minist'red.[179]

It is *this* nature which, "stronger than his just occasion,"[180] later causes Orlando to save his sleeping brother from a lioness.

The play's "savage" humans are all solitary: the two wicked brothers, made lonely by their greed and violence, and the "one man" of Jaques' speech on the seven ages. Jaques' detachment, since it is a detachment from his own kind, can only be cynical. His point of view is resolutely ontogenetic; he gives the life history of a lone specimen, made utterly destitute by old age: "second childishness and mere oblivion, / Sans teeth, sans eyes, sans taste, sans everything."[181] And these lines are immediately followed by phylogeny, history, community, all that holds the possibility of meaning for humans—surely the most eloquent and moving of stage directions: "*Enter Orlando, with Adam.*"

This Adam is an old man saved from despair by the love of a young man, who has been saved from despair by the love of a young woman. And the play is spindled on the progress of the young man from hate and despair through these loves to maturity.

As You Like It may be said to be about maturity, the acceptance of a place properly human in the world as it is, and the willingness to act responsibly in that world—a maturity very close to what Pope and Jane Austen would call "sense." This maturity, as the various characters attain it or exhibit it, seems each time to be defined in opposition to the character of Jaques. The Duke's maturity is in his gentle, unsentimental willingness to live in the forest on the forest's terms. Adam's is in his double faithfulness:

> I have five hundred crowns,
> ....
> Which I did store to be my foster nurse . . .
> ....
> Take that, and he that doth the ravens feed,
> Yea, providently caters for the sparrow,
> Be comfort to my age.[182]

The shepherd Corin's maturity is in his understanding of himself as a "true laborer," and this speech of his is perhaps the standard by which we are to measure the other characters:

I earn that I eat, get that I wear, owe no man hate, envy no man's happiness, glad of other men's good, content with my harm; and the greatest of my pride is to see my ewes graze and my lambs suck.[183]

Rosalind's is defined directly in rejection of Jaques' melancholy, which, he says, is "compounded of . . . the sundry contemplation of my travels, which, by often rumination, wraps me in a most humorous sadness":

> A traveller! By my faith, you have great reason to be sad. I fear you have sold your own lands to see other men's. Then to have seen much and to have nothing is to have rich eyes and poor hands.
>
> . . . .
>
> Farewell, Monsieur Traveller. Look you lisp and wear strange suits, disable all the benefits of your own country, be out of love with your nativity, and almost chide God for making you that countenance you are . . .[184]

Orlando's maturity comes full at last when he saves and forgives his repentant brother, and rejects, for marriage, the stance of romantic lover, in which he has too much resembled Jaques: "I can live no longer by thinking."[185]

That this maturity is achieved or revealed in a wilderness causes the play to resonate within a rich cultural tradition and to awaken and renew that tradition in the minds of its audience. But this theme appears to be true, not only to its tradition, but to human nature. The human place and estate are necessarily artificial and domestic; humans have no earthly place but what they choose to make and to keep; and all domestic artifacts must sooner or later be brought back or brought down to be measured, understood, and corrected by nature. In *As You Like It*, the forest stands over and around the exiles as a teacher; it tells them what they are; it tells them what they need and what they must do, though in exile, to be at home. If they can be at home— that is, keep their *human* nature—in nature, then they are fit to return to domesticity.

But if the forest stands over them as teacher, it also stands over them as judge. If it is possible to be right, it is also possible to be wrong, and when human life is seen clearly within its inescapable natural setting, the difference shows. The key to the play is given us, then, when Touchstone says, almost as Sir Albert Howard would later say: "You have said; but whether wisely or no, let the forest judge."[186]

That such a statement could be meant with the utmost seriousness is confirmed by the trial of Mutability in *The Faerie Queene*, Book VII, in which the idea is developed fully. There Nature is called upon as a judge

> Who Right to all dost deale indifferently,
> Damning all Wrong and tortious Iniurie,
>   Which any of thy creatures doe to other
>   (Oppressing them with power, vnequally)
>   Sith of them all thou art the equall mother,
> And knittest each to each, as brother vnto brother.[187]

Nature, as I said earlier, is a hard judge, who does deal Right indifferently; ecological justice is always done, but not always immediately and not always to the guilty. But we do not have to be the victims of this indifferent justice, or not to the extent that we now are and seem likely to be. Nature's indifference is to a considerable extent mitigable by *our* concern and virtue. For she is judge not only of our acts but of our truth. If we ask her rightly the right questions, she will give us the right answers. For Nature is not a tyrant; she is, as Spenser says, the "greatest goddesse" and our "Grandmother." But she will not acknowledge her human grandchildren until we have acknowledged her and paid her our respect.

If we ask the forest how to farm—as Sir Albert Howard instructed, remembering, we may almost suppose, Shakespeare and Pope—it will tell us. And what it will tell us, as I think the great tradition represented by these poets also tells us, is that one's farm—like any other place on earth, like one's place in the order of Creation—is indeed a form. It's not a literary form, but it is *like* a literary form, and it cannot properly be ignored or its influence safely excluded by any literary form that is made within it. Like any other form, it requires us to do some things, and forbids us to do others. Some acts are fitting and becoming, and some acts are not. If we fail to do what is required and if we do what is forbidden, we exclude ourselves from the mercy of Nature; we destroy our place, or we are exiled from it. In the terms of this tradition we are "lost"—not in the wilderness, for when we are lost in this sense, when we are displaced, we are lost to the wilderness as to all else. We are lost in the "dark wood" of Dante—dark, I think, not because the wood itself is dark, but because we cannot see where we are. We are lost in our own error.

NOTES

1. *A Continuous Harmony*, Harcourt Brace Jovanovich, 1972, p. 52.
2. *Paradise Lost* I, 254–255.
3. "Under Ben Bulben."
4. *Paradiso* XXV, 40–45 (Singleton translation, here and following).
5. Lines 78–84.
6. "On Being Arrived at Twenty-three Years of Age."
7. "On His Blindness."
8. Book III, 60–62.
9. "An Apology for Smectymnuus," *The Works of John Milton*, Frank Allen Patterson, General Editor, Columbia University Press, 1931, Vol. III, page 287.
10. *Ibid.*, pages 303–304.
11. Lines 702–703.
12. *Paradiso* XXXIII, 145.
13. *Ibid.*, XXV, 67–69.
14. "Epics," *The New York Review of Books*, Feb. 21, 1980, page 4.
15. *The Works of John Milton*, Vol. IV, page 286.
16. Book 2, Chapter 3 (Jowett & Twining translation).
17. Lines 23–26, 29–32.
18. Line 3.

19. Lines 51–55.

20. Exodus 3:1–5.

21. ". . . that first proud one, who . . . through not waiting for the light, fell unripe . . ." (*Paradiso* XIX, 46, 48). But the link between pride and impatience, humility and patience, is implicit in the theology of *The Divine Comedy*, as shown, for example, by the paraphrase of Matthew 7:10 in *Purgatorio* XI, 7–9: "May the peace of Thy kingdom come to us, for we cannot reach it of ourselves. . . ." It is implicit in the narrative of the *Paradiso*: the ascent is by "steps," the higher dependent upon the lower. And it is the implicit justification of the art of the poem. Art is the necessary difficulty interposed between the seeker and the Truth, so that the ascent will not be too swift: "Far worse than in vain does he leave the shore . . . who fishes for the truth and has not the art." (*Paradiso* XIII, 121, 123.)

22. *Lives of the Poets*, Oxford (The World's Classics), Vol. I, page 109.

23. Lines 167, 172–175.

24. Line 24.

25. Line 23.

26. Dr. Johnson called it "an inconvenience of Milton's design . . . that it requires the description of what cannot be described. . . ." *Lives of the Poets*, Oxford (The World's Classics), Vol. I, page 127.

27. William Blake, *The Marriage of Heaven and Hell*, Plates 5–6 (Keynes edition).

28. *Ibid.*

29. "A Defence of Poetry," *Selected Poetry, Prose and Letters*, Edited by A. S. B. Glover, The Nonesuch Press, 1951, page 1044.

30. *Henryson*, Penguin Books, 1973, pages 10–11.

31. *Paradiso* XXXIII, 55–63.

32. *Paradiso* XXVIII, 16–18.

33. *Paradiso* XXIV, 23–25.

34. Lines 14–24.

35. Lines 31–32.

36. Lines 39–41.

37. Lines 46–47.

38. Lines 66–67.

39. Lines 720–729.

40. Lines 762–779.

41. It is, I am afraid, now conceivable that someone will argue that

"beseeming share" is a quantity humanistically determinable—that is, *all* nature equally divided among all humans. But that, obviously, is neither Biblical, moral, ecological, healthful, nor a possible definition of *temperance*.

42. Lines 896–897.
43. Line 815.
44. Lines 803–804.
45. Lines 691–692, 705–708, 716–717.
46. Vala, IX, 709.
47. Book IX, 817–825.
48. Lines 172–175.
49. *To the Palace of Wisdom*, Southern Illinois University Press, 1964, p. 64.
50. Lines 372–373, 376–377.
51. Lines 400–405.
52. Lines 429–432, 443–444, 449–450.
53. Lines 297–300.
54. Lines 301–304.
55. Line 369.
56. The First Part, lines 62–63.
57. The First Part, lines 452–455, 462–465, 517–518.
58. The Second Part, lines 164–167.
59. The Second Part, lines 182–187, 189–194.
60. The Second Part, lines 483–484.
61. The First Part, lines 118–119, 122–123, 126–127, 146–148.
62. Lines 469–487.
63. Lines 651–654.
64. Epistle I, lines 17–22.
65. The First Part, lines 274–279.
66. *An Essay on Man*, III, 148.
67. *The Faerie Queene*, IIII, VI, xxiv.
68. IIII, VI, xxxi.
69. IIII, VII, v.
70. Sierra Club Books, 1980, pages 3, 11–15, 30, 33, 282.
71. *Lives of the English Poets*, Oxford (The World's Classics), Vol. II, page 323.
72. *Op. cit.*, page 21.
73. Epistle I, lines 237–241.
74. Epistle I, lines 244–250.
75. Epistle I, lines 257–258.
76. Lines 15–18, 21–25.

77. Epistle III, lines 311–312.
78. Epistle II, line 1.
79. *Op. cit.*, page 22.
80. *Ibid.*, page 15.
81. Epistle I, lines 113–122.
82. Peter Quennell, *Alexander Pope: The Education of Genius, 1688–1728*, Stein and Day, 1970, pages 216, 228.
83. Epistle I, lines 123–128.
84. Epistle I, lines 267–275.
85. *Op. cit.*, page 217.
86. Epistle IV, lines 49–50.
87. V, II, xxx.
88. V, II, xxxiii.
89. V, II, xxxvi.
90. V, II, xxxvii–xxxviii.
91. V, II, xxxix.
92. V, II, xl–xli.
93. V, II, xliv.
94. V, II, xix.
95. All quotations and information about Pope as gardener in this paragraph are from Quennell, *op. cit.*, pages 178–187.
96. Book V, lines 211–216.
97. Lines 50, 57.
98. *The Country and the City*, Oxford, 1975, page 123.
99. Line 64.
100. Lines 225, 233.
101. Lines 9–62.
102. "The Manichaeans," *The Back Country*, New Directions, 1967, page 76.
103. One kind of compositional unit in Mr. Snyder's work is a mimetic structure involving sight, sound, and movement:

    never a leader,
    all of one swift

    empty
    dancing   mind.

    They arc and loop & then
    their flight is done.
    they settle down.

("Straight-Creek–Great Burn," *Turtle Island*, New Directions, 1974, page 53.)

The notion that Pope is rigidly formal and rational may prevent one from seeing instances of *this* sort of formality in him:

> The spider's touch, how exquisitely fine!
> Feels at each thread, and lives along the line . . .
> (*An Essay on Man*, Epistle I, lines 217–218.)

104. *The Real Work*, edited with an introduction by Wm. Scott McLean, New Directions, 1980, page 82.
105. *An Essay on Man*, Epistle III, lines 119–121.
106. *An Agricultural Testament*, Oxford University Press, 1956, page 4.
107. *New Roots for Agriculture*, Friends of the Earth, 1981.
108. "Tomorrow Is Our Permanent Address," *The Book of the New Alchemists*, edited by Nancy Jack Todd, E. P. Dutton, 1977, pages 114–130.
109. *Where Man Belongs*, Collins (London), 1946, page 240.
110. *Epistle to Burlington*, lines 41–45.
111. Lines 65–70.
112. Lines 15–16, 19–22.
113. *The Spirit of the Age*, Oxford (The World's Classics), 1970, page 133.
114. "On Shakespeare and Milton," *Lectures on the English Poets*, Russell & Russell, 1968, pages 100–101.
115. "On the Living Poets," *ibid*., page 312.
116. *Ibid*., page 311.
117. *Op. cit*., page 1049.
118. Lines 172–176.
119. *Op. cit*., page 1052.
120. *Ibid*., page 1052.
121. *Ibid*., page 1027.
122. *Ibid*., page 1027.
123. *Ibid*., page 1047.
124. *Ibid*., page 1049.
125. Lines 149–153.
126. Line 159.
127. Lines 160–161.
128. Quoted by Edward Dowden, "Introduction," *The Complete Poetical Works of Percy Bysshe Shelley*, Thomas Y. Crowell, n.d., page 15.

129. Lines 174–177.

130. Lines 178–181.

131. Lines 415–417.

132. *Op. cit.*, page 1042.

133. Line 457.

134. Lines 565–568.

135. Line 591.

136. "Advertisement" preceding *Epipsychidion*.

137. Stanzas XVIII, XX.

138. "On Mr. Wordsworth's 'Excursion,' " *Lectures on the English Poets*, page 345.

139. "*Prometheus Unbound*," *Essays and Introductions*, Macmillan, 1961, pages 423, 424.

140. *The Outline of Sanity*, Dodd, Mead, 1927, page 76.

141. *The Pound Era*, University of California Press, second printing, 1973, pages 558, 560.

142. Canto XLV, *The Cantos*, Faber and Faber, 1964, pages 239–240.

143. "On Mr. Wordsworth's 'Excursion,' " *Lectures on the English Poets*, pages 352–353.

144. William Wordsworth, *The Poetical Works*, edited by E. de Sélincourt and Helen Darbishire, Oxford, 1949, Vol. 5, pages 3–6, lines 47–51.

145. *Ibid.*, lines 19–22.

146. *Ibid.*, lines 25–41.

147. "On Mr. Wordsworth's 'Excursion,' " *Lectures on the English Poets*, page 356.

148. *An Essay on Man*, II, lines 19–26, 29–30.

149. *The Prelude*, VIII, lines 223–229.

150. *Ibid.*, lines 101–110.

151. *Ibid.*, lines 275–276.

152. *Ibid.*, VI, lines 513–514.

153. *The Excursion*, I, lines 77–80.

154. Wordsworth and Coleridge, *Lyrical Ballads*, 1798, edited by W. J. B. Owen, Oxford, 1967, page 161.

155. Lines 12–14, 16–20, 23–25.

156. I am drawing a likeness here, not an analogy. I am not saying that male is wild and female domestic, or vice versa.

157. Canto LXXXI, *op. cit.*, p. 556.

158. "Milton," *op. cit.*, Vol. I, p. 112.

159. VI, II, i.

160. VI, IX, xviii.

161. VI, IX, xx.

162. *Op. cit.*, p. 116.

163. VI, IX, xxix, xxx.

164. VI, IX, xxiv.

165. VI, X, xi.

166. Ralph M. Sargent, editor, Penguin Books, 1970, I, i, 9–14.

167. I, i, 34–35.

168. I, i, 74.

169. I, ii, 170–176.

170. II, i, 3–4.

171. II, i, 10–11.

172. II, i, 15–17.

173. "And the Life Was the Light of Men," from the *Homily on the Prologue to the Gospel of St. John*, translated by Christopher Bamford, in *Celtic Christianity*, Lindisfarne Letter No. 13, Lindisfarne Press, 1982, page 78.

174. II, i, 21–25.

175. II, i, 61–63.

176. V, iv, 102–104.

177. Albert C. Baugh, editor, *A Literary History of England*, Second Edition, Prentice-Hall, 1948, page 526.

178. II, vii, 167–168.

179. II, vii, 120–126.

180. IV, iii, 130.

181. II, vii, 165–166.

182. II, iii, 38, 40, 43–45.

183. III, ii, 69–73.

184. IV, i, 15, 17–22, 30–34.

185. V, ii, 48.

186. III, ii, 116–117.

187. VII, VII, xiv.

Poetry and Marriage:
The Use of Old Forms (1982)

The meaning of marriage begins in the giving of words. We cannot join ourselves to one another without giving our word. And this must be an unconditional giving, for in joining ourselves to one another we join ourselves to the unknown. We can join one another *only* by joining the unknown. We must not be misled by the procedures of experimental thought: in life, in the world, we are never given two known results to choose between, but only *one* result that we choose without knowing what it is.

Marriage rests upon the immutable *givens* that compose it: words, bodies, characters, histories, places. Some wishes cannot succeed; some victories cannot be won; some loneliness is incorrigible. But there is relief and freedom in knowing what is real; these givens come to us out of the perennial reality of the world, like the terrain we live on. One does not care for this ground to make it a different place, or to make it perfect, but to make it inhabitable and to make it better. To flee from its realities is only to arrive at them unprepared.

Because the condition of marriage is worldly and its meaning communal, no one party to it can be solely in charge. What you alone think it ought to be, it is not going to be. Where you alone think you want it to go, it is not going to go. It is going where the two of you—and marriage, time, life, history, and the world—will take it. You do not know the road; you have committed your life to a way.

In marriage as in poetry, the given word implies the acceptance of a form that is never entirely of one's own making. When understood seriously enough, a form is a way of accepting and of living within the limits of creaturely life. We live only one life, and die only one death. A marriage cannot include everybody, because the reach of responsibility is short. A poem cannot be about everything, for the reach of attention and insight is short.

There are two aspects to these forms. The first is the *way* of making or acting or doing, which is to some extent technical. That is to say that definitions—settings of limits—are involved. The names *poetry* and *marriage* are given only to certain things, not to anything or to everything. Poetry is made of words; it is expected to keep a certain fidelity to everyday speech and a certain fidelity to music; if it is unspeakable or unmusical, it is not poetry. Marriage is the mutual promise of a man and a woman to live together, to love and help each other, in mutual fidelity, until death. It is understood that these definitions cannot be altered to suit convenience or circumstance, any more than we can call a rabbit a squirrel because we preferred to see a squirrel. Poetry of the traditionally formed sort, for instance, does not propose that its difficulties should be solved by skipping or forcing a rhyme or by mutilating syntax or by writing prose. Marriage does not invite one to solve one's quarrel with one's wife by marrying a more compliant woman. Certain limits, in short, are prescribed—imposed *before* the beginning.

The second aspect of these forms is an opening, a generosity, toward possibility. The forms acknowledge that good is possible; they hope for it, await it, and prepare its welcome—though they dare not *require* it. These two aspects are inseparable. To forsake the way is to forsake the possibility. To give up the form is to abandon the hope.

A certain awesome futurity, then, is the inescapable condition of word-giving—as it is, in fact, of all speech—for we speak into no future that we know, much less into one that we desire, but into one that is unknown. But that it is unknown requires us to be generous toward it, and requires our generosity to be full and unconditional. The unknown is the mercy and it may be the redemption of the known. The given word may come to appear to be wrong, or wrongly given. But the unknown still lies ahead of it, and so who is finally to say? If time has apparently proved it wrong, more time may prove it right. As growth has called it into question, further growth may reaffirm it.

These forms are artificial; if they exist they have to be made. Sexual love is natural, but marriage is not. The impulse to sing is natural, but language and the forms of song are not.

These forms are also initially arbitrary, because at the outset they can always be argued against. Until the wedding vows are said, the argument that one might find a better spouse has standing because there is no argument or evidence that can be produced against it; statistical probability would seem to support it: given the great number of theoretically possible choices, one *might* make a better choice. The vows answer that argument simply by cloture: the marriage now exists beyond all possibility of objection. A vow, Beatrice says, in *Paradiso* V, "is never canceled save by being kept . . . ," and must not be changed or broken on one's own judgment, though her stricture does not apply to vows that are foolish or perverse like those of Jephthah and Agamemnon. (She is acknowledging, let me emphasize, that some vows *ought* to be broken. Undoubtedly, some marriages are wrong, some divorces right. But it must also be understood, I think, that the possibility of breaking a vow can tell us nothing of what is meant by making and keeping one. Divorce is the contradiction of marriage, not one of its proposed results.)

Similarly, before the poem, there is no necessity governing the choice of form. Why *The Faerie Queene* should have been written in Spenserian stanzas is an unanswerable and probably a pointless question. All we can do is acknowledge that it *is* so written and go on to questions that are answerable.

The forms, then, are arbitrary *before* they are entered upon. Afterward, they have the same undoubtable existence and standing as the forms of an elm or a river. A poet such as Spenser evidently entered upon the form of a poem as solemnly as he entered upon any other cultural form—that of public service, say, or that of marriage. He understood it both as enablement and as constraint, and he meant not to break it, for in keeping the form he did not merely obey an arbitrarily imposed technical requirement but maintained his place in his cultural lineage, as both inheritor and bequeather, which saved him from loneliness and enabled him to mean—as witness his filial apostrophe to Chaucer in *The Faerie Queen*:

> through infusion sweete
> Of thine owne spirit, which doth in me survive
> I follow here the footing of thy feete,
> That with thy meaning so I may the rather meete.

(Though my concern here is with *making*, I should point out that the reader of a poem also participates in its form and in the community it makes, precisely as Spenser says: by following the footing of the poet's feet.)

Arbitrary in the choosing, these forms, once chosen and kept, are not arbitrary, but become inseparable from our definition as human beings. But the decision to break them is again arbitrary, for it cannot be based on any sufficient argument or evidence. And this decision does not return us to the state (perfectly inhabitable and respectable) that we were in before we chose the form but throws us into a state of formlessness, which is painful and dangerous, and which we can escape only by a return to form. The choice of a form is rightly solemn, both because of the gravity of the responsibility to keep it and because of the danger of failing to keep it. This choice does not present itself in any way that we may safely take less than seriously. To have a life or a place or a poem that is formless—into which anything at all may, or may not, enter—is to be condemned, at best, to bewilderment.

It is often assumed, as if under the influence of the promises of advertisements, that need or desire, ambition or inspiration may proceed straight to satisfaction. But this is false, contrary to the nature of form and the nature of discipline, as it is to common experience. It may sometimes happen by chance, but it does not dependably happen by chance. When it happens by luck, it will generally be found to be the luck of the well prepared. These impulses dependably come to fruition only by encountering the resistances of form, by being balked, baffled, forced to turn back and start again. They come to fruition by error and correction. Form is the means by which error is recognized and the means by which correctness is recognized.

There are, it seems, two Muses: the Muse of Inspiration, who gives us inarticulate visions and desires, and the Muse of Realization, who returns again and again to say, "It is yet more difficult than you thought." This is the muse of form.

The first muse is the one mainly listened to in a cheap-energy civilization, in which "economic health" depends on the assumption that everything desirable lies within easy reach of anyone. To hear the second muse one must move outside the cheap-energy enclosure. It is the willingness to hear the second muse that keeps us cheerful in our work. To hear only the first is to live in the bitterness of disappointment.

It is true that any form can be applied with a stupid rigidity. It can be falsely exclusive, consigning all that it cannot contain "to cold oblivion," as Shelley wrongly believed marriage was supposed to do. A set verse form can, of course, be used like a cookie cutter or a shovel, including and excluding arbitrarily by its own rule. But a set form can be used also to summon into a poem, or into a life, its unforeseen belongings, and thus is not rigid but freeing—an invocation to unknown possibility.

Form, crudely or stupidly used, may indeed be inimical to freedom. Well used, it may be the means of earning freedom, the price of admission or permission, the enablement to be free. But the connection may be even closer, more active and interesting, than that; it may be that form, strictly kept, *enforces* freedom. The form can be fulfilled only by a kind of abandonment to hope and to possibility, to unexpected gifts. The argument for freedom is not an argument against form. Form, like topsoil (which is intricately formal), empowers time to do good.

Properly used, a verse form, like a marriage, creates impasses, which the will and present understanding can solve only arbitrarily and superficially. These halts and difficulties do not ask for immediate remedy; we fail them by making emergencies of them. They ask, rather, for patience, forbearance, inspiration—the gifts and graces of time, circumstance, and faith. They are, perhaps, the true occasions of the poem: occasions for surpassing what we know or have reason to expect. They are points of growth, like the axils of leaves. Writing in a set form, rightly understood, is anything but force and predetermination. One puts down the first line of the pattern *in trust* that life and language are abundant enough to complete it. Rightly understood, a set form prescribes its restraint to the poet, not to the subject.

Marriage too is an attempt to rhyme, to bring two different lives—within the one life of their troth and household—periodically into agreement or consent. The two lives stray apart necessarily, and by consent come together again: to "feel together," to "be of the same mind." Difficult virtues are again necessary. And failure, permanent failure, is possible. But it is this possibility of failure, together with the formal bounds, that turns us back from fantasy, wishful thinking, and self-pity into the real terms and occasions of our lives.

It may be, then, that form serves us best when it works as an obstruction to baffle us and deflect our intended course. It may be that when we no longer know what to do we have come to our real work and that when we no longer know which way to go we have begun our real journey. The mind that is not baffled is not employed. The impeded stream is the one that sings.

In this way the keeping of the form instructs us. We had been prepared to learn what we had the poor power to expect. But fidelity to the form has driven us beyond expectation. The world, the truth, is more abounding, more delightful, more demanding than we thought. What appeared for a time perhaps to be mere dutifulness, that dried skull, suddenly breaks open in sweetness—and we are not where we thought we were, nowhere that we could have expected to be. It was expectation that would have kept us where we were.

In *Taking the Path of Zen*, Robert Aitken Roshi says: "It is not unusual to find true resonance with a so-called advanced koan in just a single dokusan, though often more time is necessary, and sometimes one gets stuck, and must stay there for a while." That necessity to "stay there for a while" is the gist of the meaning of form. Forms join us to time, to the consequences and fruitions of our own passing. The Zen student, the poet, the husband, the wife—none knows with certainty what he or she is staying for, but all know the likelihood that they will be staying "a while": to find out what they are staying for. And it is the faith of all of these disciplines that they will not stay to find that they should not have stayed.

That faith has nothing to do with what is usually called optimism. As the traditional marriage ceremony insists, not everything that we stay to find out will make us happy. The faith, rather, is that by staying, and only by staying, we will learn something of the truth, that the truth is good to know, and that it is always both different and larger than we thought.

The exploiter and the Shelleyan romantic (who are often the same person) are always in flight from consequence, the troubles of duration. The religious disciple, the husband and wife, the poet, like the true husbandman, accept the duration and effort, even the struggle, of formal commitment. They must come prepared to stay; if they mean to stay they will have to work, and they must learn the difference between good work and bad—which is to say that the capability of good work must be handed down from old to young.

The filial piety of Spenser, following the footing of the feet of Chaucer, has its opposite in the character of Michael in Eliot's *The Elder Statesman*, who longs to be fatherless in a present "freed" from the past, so that his name will be, as we say, "just a word":

> I simply want to lead a life of my own,
> According to my own ideas of good and bad,
> Of right and wrong. I want to go far away
> To some country where no one has heard the name of Claverton . . .

We will find that dream of escape in Shelley, who might be surprised—though *we* should not be—to discover that what Michael wants to do with his freedom is

>   to go abroad
> As a partner in some interesting business.
> . . . .
>   Import and export,
> With opportunity of profits both ways.

Part of the nature of a form seems to be that it is communal—that it can be bequeathed and inherited, that it can be taught, not as an instance (a relic), but as a way still usable. Both its validity and its availability depend upon our common understanding that we humans are all fundamentally alike.

Forms are broken, usually, on the authority of the opposing principle that we are all fundamentally or essentially different. Each individual, each experience, each life is assumed to be unique—hence, each individual should be "free" to express or fulfill his or her unique self in a way appropriately unique.

Both the communal and the individual emphases can be carried to extremes, and the extremity of each is loneliness. One can be lonely in the totalitarian crowd, in which no difference is perceived or tolerated; and one can be lonely in the difference or uniqueness of individuality in which community is repudiated.

The whole range of possibilities can be exemplified within language itself. It is possible to speak a language so commonized by generality or jargon or slang that one's own mind and life virtually disappear into it. And it is possible to speak a language made so personal by contrivance, affectation, or slovenliness that one makes no sense. Between the two are the Confucian principles dear to Pound of fidelity ("the man . . . standing by his word") and sincerity (precise speech: words that can be stood by).

This word-keeping, standing by one's word, is a double fidelity: to the community and to oneself. It is the willingness of difference both to represent itself and to account for itself. The individual is thereby at once free and a member. To break one's word in order to be "free" of it, on the other hand, is to make and enforce a damning equation between freedom and loneliness.

The freedom that depends upon or results in the breaking of words and the breaking of forms comes, I think, from a faith in the individual intelligence, in "genius," as opposed to a faith in the community or in culture. Belief in culture calls for the same disciplines as belief in marriage. It calls, indeed, for *more* patience and *more* faith, for it requires dedication to work and hope of more than a lifetime. This work, as I understand it, consists of the accumulation of local knowledge *in place*, generation after generation, children learning the visions and failures, stories and songs, names, ways, and skills of their elders, so that the costs of individual trial-and-error learning can be lived with and repaid, and the community thus enabled to preserve both itself and its natural place and neighborhood.

I do not mean that the rebellions of genius are necessarily bad; they may be both inevitable and indispensable. But they *can* be bad; they are dangerous, and it is prudent to understand what their dangers are. We may be properly suspicious of them when they are carried out in the name of "personal freedom" or "personal fulfillment," and when their program is a general rebellion against the imperfect past.

"Freedom" and "fulfillment" are often coupled together in the idea that one must be free in order to fulfill oneself. Behind the divorce epidemic—as behind the epidemics of venereal disease and accidental parenthood among the young—is the unappeasable demon of "sexual fulfillment." Behind the epidemic of poetic illiteracy is the conviction that one must free oneself from poetic tradition (by not learning it) in order to fulfill one's ambition. The question here is whether we want "fulfill" to mean more than "satisfy"—as it must if we take seriously even its literal sense: to fill full. Sexual desire is an appetite, and so, in a different way, is ambition; they can be fulfilled only temporarily and soon have to be refulfilled. Though we would like it to be, "sexual fulfillment" is really no more exalted an idea than "hunger fulfillment." Ambition fulfillment, as we still understand when talking of politics or war, is a dangerous enterprise—for a mental appetite may be larger and more rapacious than a physical one, may require to be refulfilled more frequently and is less likely to be twice appeased by the same refulfillment.

If we mean "fulfill" in its larger sense—to discharge or put to rest, as when one fulfills an obligation or a promise—then we see that what we fulfill are not appetites but forms. Marriage is a form of sexual love which allows its fulfillment in both senses: in satisfaction and in responsibility for its consequences, and it sets a term to this responsibility—"until death"—at which it may be said to be fulfilled. The form of a particular poem similarly allows a valid fulfillment of poetic ambition. And the particularity of these fulfillments, working as they do to define complex obligations to discipline, to community, to tradition, to forebears and successors, mitigates the dangers of self-renewing appetites. The seriousness of this formality can hardly be overstated, for in the fulfillment of form is death—as the marriage vows instruct us. Fulfillment "bears it out even to the edge of doom." Past fulfillment, desire is at an end; there is no need to return. Great cost is obviously involved. But to stop short of such fulfillment is to make love "time's fool," and to fix a value upon a worth unknown.

Outrage and rebellion against the past are undoubtedly human necessities, but they are limited necessities, and they probably should be limited to youth. Things are obviously wrong with the past; young people have the clarity to see them and the energy to rebel against them. But as a general principle, such rebellion is destructive, for it keeps us from seeing that the past, unsatisfactory as it is, is the source of nearly all our good. Maturity sees that the past is not to be rejected, destroyed, or replaced, but rather that it is to be judged and corrected, that the work of judgment and correction is endless, and that it necessarily involves one's *own* past.

The industrial economy has made a general principle of the youthful antipathy to the past, and the modern world abounds with heralds of "a better future" and with debunkers happy to point out that Yeats was "silly like us" or that Thomas Jefferson may have had a Negro slave as a mistress—and so we are disencumbered of the burden of great lives, set free to be as cynical or desperate as we please. Cultural forms, it is held, should change apace to keep up with technology. Sexual discipline should be replaced by the chemicals, devices, and procedures of "birth control," and poetry must hasten to accept the influence of typewriter or computer.

It can be better argued that cultural forms ought to change by analogy with biological forms. I assume that they *do* change in that way, and by the same necessity to respond to changes of circumstance. It is necessary, nevertheless, to recognize a difference in kinds of cultural change: there is change by necessity, or adaptation; and there is contrived change, or novelty. The first is the work of species or communities or lineages of descent, occurring usually by slow increments over a long time. The second is the work of individual minds, and it happens, or is intended to happen, by fiat. Individual attempts to change cultural form—as to make a new kind of marriage or family or community—are nearly always shallow or foolish and are frequently totalitarian. The assumption that it can easily be otherwise comes from the faith in genius.

To adopt a communal form with the idea of changing or discarding it according to individual judgment is hopeless, the despair and death of meaning. To keep the form is an act of faith in possibility, not of the form, but of the life that is given to it; the form is a question addressed to life and time, which only life and time can answer.

Individual genius, then, goes astray when it proposes to do the work of community. We rightly follow its promptings, on the other hand, when it can point out correctly that *we* have gone astray—when forms have become rigid or empty, when we have forgot their use or their meaning. We then follow our genius or our geniuses back to reverence, to truth, or to nature. This alternation is one of the long rhythms of our history.

But the faith in genius and the rebellions of genius, at the times when these are necessary, should lead to the renewal of forms, not to their destruction. No individual can justifiably destroy anything of communal value on behalf of the community. Though individual geniuses have often enough assumed otherwise, there is no reason to grant them special privileges or exemptions. No artistic or scientific genius is justified in abusing nature or culture.

The analogy I have been working with here is most readily apparent if we think of marriage and poetic forms as *set* forms—that is, forms that in a sense *precede* the content, that are in a sense *prescriptive*. These set forms are indispensable, I believe, because they accommodate and serve that part of our life which is cyclic, drawing minds and lives back repeatedly through the same patterns, as each year moves through the same four seasons in the same order.

My remaining problem is to see how so-called free verse may fit into my scheme. It *has* to be fitted in if I am to respect my scheme, and if I acknowledge, as I certainly do, that much free verse is poetry. There is some danger of becoming cute or precious in carrying this analogy out to such length, and yet I am working on the assumption that the analogy is valid.

One analogue of free verse, I think, must be courtship, a way of accommodating our minds to something new, of finding out what it is that we are doing or about to do. The encounter be-tween the English language and the subjects and objects of a new continent strange to it and to its poetic tradition seems to have required this of a succession of American poets from Whitman's time until now. Who can help feeling in the early *Leaves of Grass* a kind of falling in love? The lines must reach out impulsively, become capacious and tensile, to include in their full stance and particularity the images of American experience:

> The negro that drives the long dray of the stone-yard,
>   steady and tall he stands pois'd on one leg on the
>   string-piece...

Never mind that these loving inventories have occurred in po-etry before. This is new, this confrontation with a continent needing to be realized, and we grant Whitman his liberty and his exultation; we feel ourselves free and exultant with him; we will-ingly forgive the absurdities that occasionally jeopardize his ex-uberance—his ostentatious French phrases, for instance, or his industrial optimism.

But if Whitman's work is the prime example of the freeing of verse, it is an example of something else too, for at its best Whit-man's line, as we will see if we try to shorten or lengthen it, is a form. He set his line free only to make it into a *kind* of line that we recognize anywhere we see it—a new power, a new music, added to poetry, which can be learned and used. Theoretically, I suppose, any line can be written a different way, but I don't think that we are tempted to imagine this line as anything but what it is:

> Seasons pursuing each other the plougher ploughs, the
>   mower mows, and the winter-grain falls in the ground...

And such newness does not destroy the old set forms, but renews them in renewing our understanding of what a line of verse is, our sense of its properties of duration and coherence, beginning and end. The term "organic," when applied to free or "open" poetic forms, should alert us to the nature of all form, traditional or new, for the organic forms of nature, like the ballad stanza or the stanza of Spenser, are principles that are repeatable and recognizable through a series of variations. This recognizability within difference suggests the proper relation of abstraction and particularity—and suggests, moreover, that the right function of abstraction is to give appropriate clarity and distinction to the particular. The form, recognizable from verse to verse, shapes and measures what is said, makes it musical.

So it is with Whitman's line. So it is, I believe, with the line of every writer of free verse worth reading. At some point the poet ceases to be an experimenter or innovator and begins a life's work. *Leaves of Grass* answers for itself the questions that stood before *The Divine Comedy* or *The Canterbury Tales*: What can be done in this way? What *must* be done in this way? Once a way is chosen with enough seriousness, the analogy shifts from courtship to marriage.

The work of poetic form is coherence, joining things that need to be joined, as marriage joins them—in words by which a man or a woman can stand, words confirmable in acts. Forms join, and this is why forms tend to be analogues of each other and to resonate with each other. Forms join the diverse things that they contain; they join their contents to their context; they join us to themselves; they join us to each other; they join writers and readers; they join the generations together, the young and the old, the living and the dead. Thus, for a couple, marriage is an entrance into a timeless community. So, for a poet (or a reader), is the mastery of poetic form. Joining the form, we join all that the form has joined.

Design by David Bullen
Typeset in Mergenthaler Sabon
by Wilsted & Taylor
Printed by Maple-Vail
on acid-free paper